Phonetics and Phonology

of Modern German

An Introduction

Wilbur A. Benware

Georgetown University Press, Washington, D.C.

Library of Congress Cataloging in Publication Data

Benware, Wilbur A.
    Phonetics and phonology of modern German.

    Includes bibliographies and index.
    1. German language—Phonetics. 2. German language—
Phonology. 3. German language—Text-books for foreign
speakers—English. I. Title.
PF3135.B46 1986   431'.5   85-7683
ISBN 0-87840-193-8

λογος δυναστης μεγας
—*Georgias of Leontini*

Contents

Preface

This book has been written with the student of German in mind who has had little or no prior linguistic training. For him/her the book provides an introduction to phonetics and phonological analysis with German as the language under investigation. It is pitched primarily at undergraduates, but graduate students in German with little linguistic knowledge will also find it useful.

Two remarks on what the book does not attempt to do: It is not orthoepical in approach, although it can be used in classes where practical problems of pronunciation are treated. A number of books are (or were) in print on orthoepy for English-speaking learners of German, for example, *Deutsche Hochlautung,* by Ursula Kreuzer and Klaus Pawlowski (Stuttgart: Klett Verlag), which can supplement the text. It is not contrastive in approach on the order of William G. Moulton's *The Sounds of English and German,* although it could be used in a comparative study of the two languages.

A number of solid introductions to German phonology already exist, such as those by Klaus J. Kohler and Gottfried Meinhold and Eberhard Stock. All are, of course, in German, and for the most part are simply too demanding for the average American undergraduate. The present book attempts to make the phonetics of Standard German, as well as a phonological analysis of it, accessible to this group. The variety of German investigated is what is often designated as 'gemäßigte Hochlautung'. For the most part, the phonetic transcriptions are consonant with those in *Duden, Aussprachewörterbuch* and *Wörterbuch der deutschen Aussprache.*

Each chapter is followed by a number of problems, which require the student to apply the material in the chapter to new data. The problems are arranged in order of difficulty, so that those which appear last require some degree of linguistic sophistication.

Acknowledgments

A number of people have contributed to the making of this book. Carol Wall of the University of California, Davis, scrutinized the chapters on phonetics and made a number of useful comments. Herbert Penzl, professor emeritus at the University of California, Berkeley, made numerous suggestions for change and improvements which were incorporated in the final draft. Needless to say, neither is responsible for the final outcome. Substantial contributions were also made by students at the University of California, Davis, whose critiques of an earlier version led to substantial revisions. To typists Michele Van Vranken and Kay Yeager go special thanks for a careful and conscientious job on a very difficult manuscript.

Introduction

The purpose of language is to transmit meaning from one person to another. The most usual way of doing this is through the medium of sound. In this book we will be examining the sounds and sound system of Modern Standard German, that variety of the language which is understood, and to a large degree used, by all persons whose native language is German.

In the following pages there are descriptions of the individual sounds as well as discussion of how the sounds of German fall into patterns. Naturally, no one can learn about the sounds of a language (or improve pronunciation) by reading a book, and the initial chapters will need a great deal of exemplification. Chapters 1-3 constitute the foundation on which the remainder of the book rests. The terminology introduced there is presupposed in all subsequent discussion. Chapters 4 through 7 treat the organization of the sound system of German, concentrating on individual sound units, whereas Chapters 10 and 11 focus on sounds in relation to syntax. The two intervening chapters (8 and 9) discuss the spelling system and the special problems related to the foreign vocabulary. The brief final chapter (12) surveys instances of the alternation of sounds in the same word.

The sound system of any language is both simple and complex. On the one hand, the number of significant sound units (phonemes) is quite limited; on the other hand, their manifold relationships to one another admit of a rich complexity. It is hoped that this book will help the student not only to gain a mastery of the German sound system, but also to appreciate its architecture and to get a feel for a linguistic method which can be applied to other languages as well.

Speak the speech, I pray you,
as I pronounc'd it to you,
trippingly on the tongue . . .
—*Shakespeare,*
Hamlet III, 2

Chapter 1
The vocal tract

1. The vocal tract. PHONETICS is the study of speech sounds, the medium
human beings employ in articulating language. In studying the sounds of a
language, one can take three basic approaches: (1) ARTICULATORY PHONET-
ICS, where the interest lies in how the various parts of the human vocal
tract are manipulated in order to produce speech sounds; (2) ACOUSTIC
PHONETICS, which investigates the physical properties of the sounds produced in the vocal tract by using various sound-recording and sound-
measuring instruments; and (3) PSYCHOACOUSTICS, which focuses on the
perception of sounds by listeners, given particular acoustic properties of
the sounds. This investigation of German phonetics concentrates almost
exclusively on the first of these possibilities. To do this, we initially look
at the form of the vocal tract and then develop a vocabulary for describing
it and its movements.

Figure 1.1 is a mid-sagittal section of the head, with those parts of the
vocal tract labeled which are important in producing speech sounds. Parts
of the vocal tract are mobile, and hence are responsible for changing its
size and shape: the larynx (often referred to in layman's terms as the
'voice box'), the velum, the tongue, and the lips. All speech sounds are
produced by blowing air from the lungs through the vocal tract and modifying its size and shape by manipulating the larynx, velum, tongue, and
lips.

The first modification of the airstream takes place at the LARYNX, a carti-
laginous structure near the top of the TRACHEA (the 'wind pipe'). The larynx contains the VOCAL CORDS or VOCAL BANDS which are composed of muscle and tissue. Figures 1.2a and 1.2b show two positions of the vocal
bands (more are possible, but for German, two suffice). In Figure 1.2a, the
vocal bands are spread apart; in Figure 1.2b, they are together. Both diagrams show the larynx as viewed from above, with the bottom of each diagram representing the front (sometimes visible as the 'Adam's apple').
The space between the vocal bands is called the GLOTTIS.

Figure 1.1 Sagittal section of the head: The vocal tract.

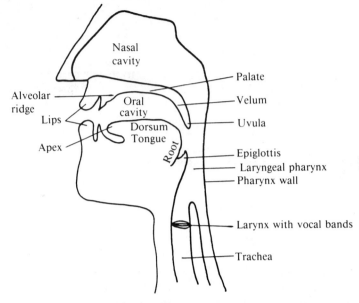

Figure 1.2.a The larynx with the vocal bands spread apart.

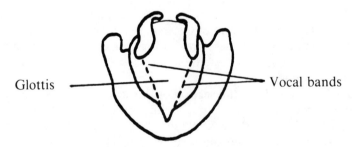

Figure 1.2b The larynx with the vocal bands together.

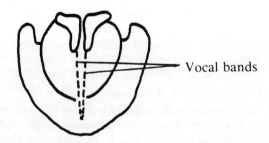

(Both diagrams after Klaus J. Kohler, *Einführung in die Phonetik des Deutschen*, p. 50; reproduced by permission of the Erich Schmidt Verlag.)

Figure 1.2a represents the position of the vocal bands in normal breathing and in the articulation of certain sounds, such as the initial sound in *Paar* and *fast,* which are termed VOICELESS. With the vocal bands together, the airstream is forced through the narrow aperture thus formed. The result is vibration of the vocal bands, producing VOICED sounds. For example, all vowel sounds in German are voiced. You can feel the difference between voiceless and voiced sounds by placing the fingertips on the front of the neck at the larynx and slowly pronouncing the initial sound in *Haar* (voiceless) and then the following vowel (voiced). You can feel the vibrations when articulating the vowel.

The airstream can also be modified by raising and lowering the larynx, resulting in an air-pressure difference between the trachea and the space above it (the SUPRAGLOTTAL cavities), but this fact is of little importance in this somewhat simplified description of the German sounds.

The size and shape of the LARYNGEAL PHARYNX can be changed by moving the ROOT of the tongue toward or away from the pharynx wall. But again, this possibility is only mentioned in passing in the following discussion.

The airstream passes into the nose or the mouth, depending on the position of the VELUM. In Figure 1.1, the velum is 'down', allowing air to pass into the nose. Sounds produced with the velum down are termed NASAL. Figure 1.3 shows the velum in the 'up' position, blocking off access to the nose. The airstream is directed into the mouth, resulting in ORAL sounds. The initial sound of *Mai,* for example, is nasal, while the initial sound of *bei* and *sah* is oral.

Figure 1.3 The vocal tract with the velum closing off the nasal cavity.

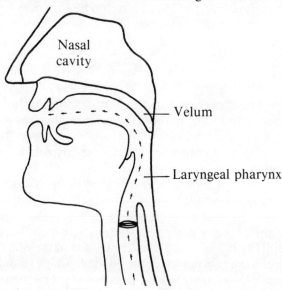

In the mouth or ORAL CAVITY, the tongue can assume a great number of different positions due to its mobility, so that most of the sounds to be investigated are described with reference to its position. Figure 1.4 represents a 'map' of the tongue's surface, with those parts labeled which are important for the description of sounds.

Figure 1.4 The surface of the tongue.

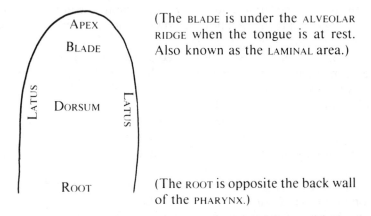

(The BLADE is under the ALVEOLAR RIDGE when the tongue is at rest. Also known as the LAMINAL area.)

(The ROOT is opposite the back wall of the PHARYNX.)

The tongue can be moved vertically, i.e. raised or lowered, and horizontally toward the front or toward the rear of the mouth, in order to touch or approach various points on the upper surface of the mouth: the TEETH, the ALVEOLAR RIDGE, the PALATE, the VELUM, and the UVULA. The alveolar ridge is the hard, somewhat rough surface behind the upper incisors. Behind it is the palate (also called the 'hard palate'). The boundary between them may be ascertained by running the thumb back from the incisors. The boundary between the palate and the velum is marked by a transition from a hard surface to a soft one. The velum ends in the uvula, the fleshy pendant hanging down in the rear of the mouth, which can easily be seen in a mirror.

Finally, the airstream can be modified by the lips, which may be unrounded or rounded. In the latter position this means a slight increase in the distance the pulmonary airstream must travel, which results in a different acoustic impression than sounds articulated when the lips are not rounded.

In summary, the airstream is modified in five ways: (1) at the larynx, by opening or closing the vocal bands; (2) in the laryngeal pharynx, by moving the root of the tongue; (3) by being directed into the oral cavity through raising the velum, or into the nasal (and oral) cavities by lowering the velum; (4) by the position of the tongue in the oral cavity; (5) by the position of the lips, rounded or unrounded. All the sounds of German can be described by referring to modifications of the airstream at these points.

Chapter 2
The vowel sounds
of German

2.0 Definition. All languages distinguish between vowels and consonants. CONSONANTS may be defined as those sounds produced by offering
some impedance to the pulmonary airstream, and vowels as those sounds
which are produced by allowing the airstream to flow unhindered through
the vocal tract.

2.1 Tongue height and tongue retraction. VOWELS are produced by raising or lowering the tongue, and at the same time bunching it under the palate or under the velum. Figure 2.1 shows the tongue in three different positions. For the articulation of the vowel in *sieh* and in *Kuh,* the tongue is
raised in comparison with the vowel in *sah.* In *sieh,* the tongue is bunched
under the palate, in *Kuh* under the velum. Little bunching (or 'retraction',
as it is called from now on) is noticeable for the vowel in *sah,* but it is clearly more velar than palatal.

   If, now, the vowel in *sieh* is represented with the symbol [i:] (where the
colon indicates that the vowel is long), that in *Kuh* by [u:], and that in *sah*
by [ɑ:], then it can be stated that [i:] and [u:] are articulated with the
tongue HIGH in the mouth when compared with [ɑ:], and that [ɑ:] is articulated LOW in the mouth in comparison with [i:] and [u:]. Or: [i:] and [u:]
are HIGH VOWELS, [ɑ:] is a LOW VOWEL. Furthermore, the tongue is bunched
more toward the front of the mouth for [i:], more toward the back for [u:]
and [ɑ:]. Or: [i:] is a FRONT vowel, [u:] and [ɑ:] are BACK vowels. Each
vowel can now be described in terms of two parameters: tongue height
and tongue retraction: [i:] is high, front; [u:] is high, back; and [ɑ:] is low,
back.

   Both parameters, of course, are relative, since we are trying to describe
the position of a body (the tongue) in a space. 'High' and 'low' are not
measured in absolute terms, say, the number of millimeters below the

5

Figure 2.1 The position of the tongue for the articulation of the three vowels [i:], [u:], [ɑ:] (after Hans-Heinrich Wängler, *Instruction in German Pronunciation*, 3rd ed.; reproduced by permission of the publisher.)

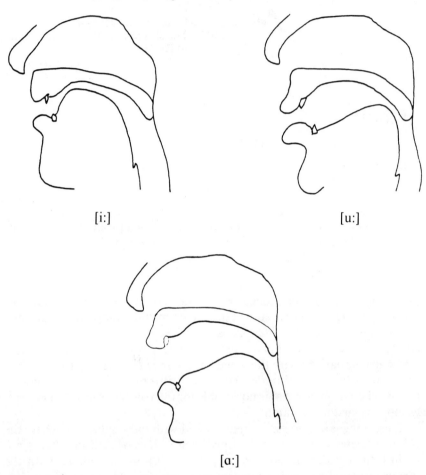

[i:]

[u:]

[ɑ:]

roof of the mouth, but are expressed relative to one another. The absolute difference between these three vowels may vary from speaker to speaker, and even from utterance to utterance in the same speaker, but the relative distance between the tongue heights enables the listener to distinguish between them.

German vowels are all voiced, that is, the vocal bands are closed and vibrate, providing a source of energy. Most vowels are oral. The velum is raised (Figure 1.3), preventing the airstream from entering the nose. Nasalized vowels, those produced with the velum down, occur in a relatively small number of words (cf. 2.2.8).

In the following discussion, the vowel sounds of German are described by using several different descriptive terms, or FEATURES. Among the features for vowels are:

(1) TONGUE HEIGHT. How far is the tongue raised toward the roof of the mouth (the palate or the velum)?

(2) TONGUE RETRACTION. Where is the tongue most bunched, toward the front (under the palate) or toward the back (under the velum)?

(3) LENGTH. The length of a vowel refers to its duration in time, and is, like the previous two terms, relative. It is only meaningful when two or more vowels can be compared. Length is indicated in the representation of sounds by placing a colon after the symbol, e.g. [i:], [u:], etc.

It is customary in phonetics to symbolize sounds by placing the relevant symbol between square brackets [   ], in order to distinguish the representation of sounds from the representation of letters of the alphabet as used in standard spelling practice. The symbols themselves are drawn from the International Phonetic Alphabet (IPA), and for the most part are those found in the pronouncing dictionaries of German.

2.2 The vowels in detail

2.2.1 The high vowels

[i:] high-front, tense, long. The vowel [i:], as has been seen, is a high-front long vowel. Figure 2.1 shows the position of the tongue for its articulation. It is the initial sound in *Igel* and *Ibis,* the medial sound in *Lieb* and *Lied,* and the final sound in *Vieh* and *Biologie.* Essential in the articulation of this vowel is the immobility of the tongue. It does not change position as is the case for the auditorily similar English vowel heard finally in *fee* and *biology.* The vowel [i:] is what is called a MONOPHTHONG (Greek *mono* 'one', *phthongos* 'sound'). The long, strictly monophthongal nature of this vowel has sometimes been attributed to strong muscular tension in the tongue and jaw, giving rise to the term 'tense'. Alongside 'high', 'front', and 'long', then, we can add the feature TENSE.

[ɪ] high-front, lax, short. The last two phonetic features stand out more clearly when the [i:], say in *Kien,* is compared with the vowel in *Kinn.* The vowel in the latter word, symbolized by [ɪ] is considerably shorter than for the articulation of [i:], and the tongue is also somewhat lower, as can be seen by the comparison of [i:] and [ɪ] in Figure 2.2. To distinguish it from the tense [i:], [ɪ] is called LAX (cf. 2.2.5 for a discussion of these terms).

[u:] high-back, tense, long, rounded. Figure 2.3 shows the position of the tongue for the articulation of [u:], which has been characterized as high, back, and long. Like its front counterpart, it is also tense. In addition, it is pronounced with the lips rounded, rather than spread apart, as is the case with [i:]. It is the initial vowel in *Uhr* and *U-Boot*, the medial sound in *Hut* and *Mus*, and the final sound in *Kuh*, *tu'*, and *Schuh*. Note once again that this vowel is a monophthong, and hence differs from the auditorily similar English vowel in *coo*, *shoe*, and *too*, which is articulated with tongue movement upward.

> *Figure 2.2* Position of the tongue for the high front vowels [i:] and [ɪ] (after Hans-Heinrich Wängler, *Instruction in German Pronunciation*, 3rd ed.; reproduced by permission of the publisher).

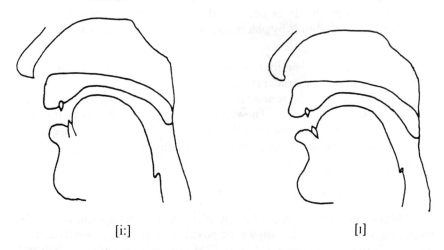

[i:]   [ɪ]

[ʊ] high-back, lax, short, rounded. The initial vowel in *und, unter,* and *uns,* and the medial vowel in *Bus, Busch,* and *Kuß,* is articulated with the tongue somewhat lower than for [u:]. It is also high and back, and shares the feature of lip-rounding with [u:]. It is lax and short. Figure 2.3 gives the typical tongue position for the articulation of [ʊ].

[y:] high-front, tense, long, rounded. It has already been noted that the front and back vowels discussed thus far differ also in lip-rounding: [i:] and [ɪ] are unrounded, [u:] and [ʊ] are rounded. German also has front, rounded vowels, as in the initial sound in *üben* and *über,* the medial sound in *kühl, Typ,* and *Süd,* and the final sound in *früh*. Like [u:], this vowel—symbolized by [y:]—is characterized by strong lip-rounding. Like [i:], it is high, front, tense, and long. Hence, the only distinguishing feature between [i:] and [y:] is lip-rounding.

[ʏ] high-front, lax, short, rounded. Just as [i:] and [u:] have their lax 'counterparts', so also has [y:]. The initial vowel in *üppig,* and the vowel in *Fürst* and *dünn,* is articulated with the tongue in the same position as for [ɪ]; cf. Figure 2.3, with the difference that this vowel is characterized by lip-rounding.

Figure 2.3 Position of the tongue for the high back vowels [u:] and [ʊ] (after Hans-Heinrich Wängler, *Instruction in German Pronunciation*, 3rd ed.; reproduced by permission of the publisher).

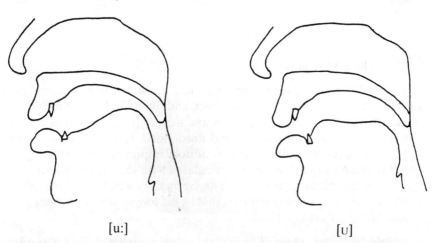

[u:]   [ʊ]

The vowels investigated so far are summarized in Table 2.1. The chart does not represent the actual position in the mouth of these vowels, however, since the shape of the oral cavity is such that the back vowels are actually lower than the front vowels when measured on a plane with the horizontal (cf. Figure 2.4).

The remainder of the 'vowel space', that area bounded by the solid line in Figure 2.4, can be divided to allow for another class of vowels, the mid vowels.

Figure 2.4 The relative tongue positions for [i:], [u:], and [ɑ:].

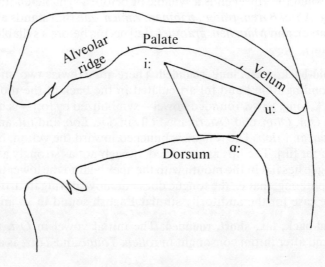

Table 2.1 The high vowels.

	Tongue retraction	Front (palate) unrounded	rounded	Back (velum) rounded	Examples
Tongue height	High Tense	[i:]	[y:]	[u:]	Kien kühl Kuh
	Lax	[ɪ]	[ʏ]	[ʊ]	Sinn dünn Bus

2.2.2 The mid vowels

[e:] mid-front, tense, long. The sound heard initially in *edel, eben,* and *Ehre,* medially in *Lehm, Mehl,* and *Beet,* and finally in *See* and *Reh,* is articulated with the tongue slightly below that of [ɪ]. Hence, it is a front vowel. Like [i:], it is long, tense, and unrounded. Its phonetic symbol is [e:]. Note that it has a quite different auditory impression than the English vowel in *lame* and *bait,* which is articulated with the tongue moving upward from an initial [e] position. The German vowel, like all the others examined so far, is a MONOPHTHONG, that is, the tongue does not change position during its articulation.

[ɛ] mid-front, lax, short. The lax, short 'counterpart' to [e:] is symbolized by [ɛ], and is heard initially in *essen, Ecke,* and *Äpfel,* medially in *fett, leck,* and *hält.* Typically, there is a greater articulatory distance between [e:] and [ɛ] than between [e:] and [ɪ]. Nonetheless, standard practice is followed here in calling both [e:] and [ɛ] mid vowels.

[ɛ:] mid-front, lax, long. The vowel symbolized by [ɛ:] is the only vowel in German which is both lax and long. Many speakers, especially in Northern Germany, do not use it at all, but prefer [e:] instead. It always corresponds to the alphabetic symbol ä (but not all ä's = [ɛ:]!). The symbol ä = [ɛ:] when the vowel ends a syllable or before a syllable-ending consonant, e.g. *Ähre, Bären, träfen, nähmen, zählen, zäh* ([ɛ:] stands at the end of a syllable), and *Mädchen, grämlich* ([ɛ:] occurs before a syllable-closing consonant).

[o:] mid-back, tense, long, rounded. There are likewise two mid vowels corresponding to [e:] and [ɛ] articulated in the back of the mouth. The mid-back, long, tense, rounded vowel—symbolized by [o:]—is heard initially in *Ohr, Ohm,* and *Ostern,* medially in *Sog, Lob,* and *tot,* and finally in *so, roh,* and *floh.* The tongue is bunched toward the velum, below the position for [u:]. The lips are rounded, though not as strongly as for [u:]. The tongue lies flat in the mouth with the apex behind the lower teeth. It is a monophthong, that is, the tongue does not move during its articulation, as is the case for the auditorily similar English sound in *so* and *flow.*

[ɔ] mid-back, lax, short, rounded. The initial vowel in *Ost, Ort,* and *Opfer,* and after initial consonant in *rollen, Tonne* and *Torte* is articulated with the tongue slightly lower than for [o:]. This vowel is also mid-back and rounded, but short and lax. Lip-rounding is not as strong as for the tense vowel [o:].

[ø:] mid-front, tense, long, rounded. Among the high vowels, it was noted that there is both a rounded and an unrounded set of front vowels. The same holds for the mid vowels. When the tongue is in approximately the position for [e:], with the lips rounded, the resulting sound is that heard initially in *öde, Öfen, Öhre,* after initial consonant in *König, töten, Bögen,* and finally in *Bö.* This vowel—symbolized by [ø:]—is thus characterized as mid-front, long, tense, and rounded.

[œ] mid-front, short, lax, rounded. This vowel is heard initially in *öfter, östlich,* and *örtlich,* and after the initial consonant of *Hölle, möchte, völlig, können, Töchter.* The tongue is in the same position as for the articulation of short, lax [ɛ].

Table 2.2 summarizes the vowels articulated with the tongue at the mid position.

Table 2.2 The mid vowels.

	Tongue retraction	Front (palate) unrounded	rounded	Back (velum) rounded	Examples	
Tongue height	Mid Tense	[e:]	[ø:]	[o:]	Besen böse	Rose
	Lax	[ɛ] [ɛ:]	[œ]	[ɔ]	essen Rößchen äßen	Roß

2.2.3 The two low vowels, short [a] and long [ɑ:]. The two low vowels, short [a] and long [ɑ:], are not distinguished as lax versus tense, as are the other pairs examined thus far. The distinction is one of length and quality (the narrowest point of constriction is actually in the laryngeal pharynx).

[a]. For [a], the initial sound in *alle, As,* and *an,* the tongue is pulled forward slightly more than for [ɑ:], the initial sound in *Aale, Aas,* and *Ahn.*

[ɑ:]. In our initial discussion [ɑ:] was classified as a back vowel. Its full description is 'low, back, long'.

The low vowel [a] is articulated with the tongue slightly more advanced, but not far enough to be called 'front'. This intermediate position between back and front is termed CENTRAL. Thus [a] is a low-central short vowel.

A final note: An examination of the three major pronouncing dictionaries of German shows that two of them use the same symbol for the low vowels, [a] and [a:]. This is the practice of *Siebs, Deutsche Aussprache* and *Der große Duden* (Band 6).*Wörterbuch der deutschen Aussprache,* on the other hand, distinguishes between [a] and [ɑ:], as has been done here. The different treatments are based on different views as to whether both length and quality are relevant when the tongue is in the lowest position. The view adopted here rests on the observation that many speakers of German do make a distinction, as x-ray evidence indicates.

2.2.4 The mid central vowels [ə] and [ɐ]. With [a] a third position has been introduced for tongue retraction between front and back. Besides [a], two other vowels in German are classified as central.

[ə]. The vowel [ə], often referred to as *schwa*, sometimes as a MURMURED VOWEL or REDUCED VOWEL, is articulated with the tongue at approximately the same height as for [e:]. It is unrounded; the apex of the tongue touches the lower teeth (compare with [ɐ]). It occurs only in unstressed syllables, e.g. finally in *Rute, Ruhe, liege, lade,* and in the last two syllables of *antwortete* and *mietetest.* It is the vowel in the prefixes *ge-* (*gemacht, Gewächs*) and *be-* (*betont, Betonung*).

[ɐ]. The vowel [ɐ] heard finally in *bitter, größer, eher, Mieter,* and *Mathematiker* is also mid-central and unrounded, but lower than [ə], tending toward a low-back position. The apex is drawn down so that it touches an area below the lower teeth. In the foregoing examples, it is unstressed. However, it commonly follows another vowel in the same stressed syllable, e.g. *Uhr* [u:ɐ] and *Ohr* [o:ɐ] (cf. 2.2.7).

Table 2.3 summarizes the discussion of the vowels thus far.

Table 2.3 The monophthongs of German. The terms 'tense' and 'lax' do not apply to [ə], [ɐ], and the low vowels.

	Tongue retraction	Front unrounded	rounded	Central	Back unrounded	rounded
Tongue height	High Tense	i:	y:			u:
	Lax	ɪ	Y			ʊ
	Mid Tense	e:	ø:	ə		o:
	Lax	ɛ ɛ:	œ	ɐ		ɔ
	Low			a	ɑ:	

2.2.5 Tense and lax vowels. The vowels represented by the symbols [ɪ Y ʊ ɛ œ ɔ] are considered 'lax' vowels. Just exactly what is referred to by the terms TENSE and LAX has been a matter of dispute. They suggest muscular tension of some sort, but this does not seem to be verified experimentally. There are clear differences, however, between the two sets. (1) The tense vowels are articulated with the body of the tongue further from the mid-central position ([ə]) than the lax vowels; cf. Figure 2.5 for typical po-

Figure 2.5 Typical tongue positions for the articulation of German monophthongs.

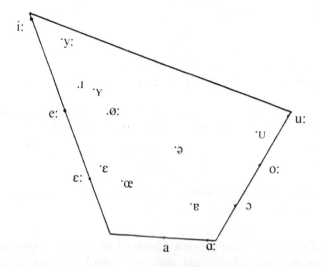

sitions. In other words, they are articulated along the periphery of the vowel space, whereas the lax vowels tend toward the center. (2) For any tense-lax pair, such as [iː] vs. [ɪ], the tense vowel is articulated with the tongue in a higher position. (3) A concomitant of (1) and (2) may be the wider pharynx due to the displacement of the tongue root toward the more extreme (tense) positions, but this characteristic seems less certain than the other two.

Table 2.3 is simply a convenient and conventional way of representing the vowels studied so far. It does not reflect the actual position of the tongue, since the articulatory space is not rectangular. Figure 2.5 shows more nearly the typical positions of the tongue in the articulation of the monophthongs.

2.2.6 Short, tense vowels. In the discussion of the monophthongs, it was stated that all tense vowels are long, all lax vowels (except [ɛː]) are short. In fact, it seemed redundant to state both length and tenseness. One entails the other. However, length is dependent on or correlated with STRESS, which is defined provisionally here as that vowel in a word which receives the greatest emphasis from the speaker and is perceived by the hearer as the most prominent. All the examples cited earlier consisted of words with tense vowels in stressed position, e.g. *Biene* [iː], *Buhle* [uː], *Besen* [eː], *böse* [øː], and *Rose* [oː].

Again, using as examples isolated words in careful pronunciation, one can find many instances of short, tense vowels, where the tense vowel is not stressed. In the following examples, the short raised perpendicular line indicates that the following syllable receives the stress:

[i:] Mor'b*i*d   [i] Morb*i*di'tät
[e:] 'leben   [e] le'bendig
[u:] Har'p*u*ne   [u] harp*u*'nieren
[o:] 'D*o*sis   [o] d*o*'sieren
[ø:] Fran'zösisch   [ø] franzö'sieren
[y:] T*y*p   [y] t*y*pi'sieren

Likewise, the two vowels [ɛ:] and [ɑ:] are long only when stressed. Long [ɛ:] becomes [ɛ], long [ɑ:] becomes [a], when unstressed.

[ɛ:] 'Dämon   [ɛ] dä'monisch
[ɑ:] Gr*a*d   [a] gra'dieren

The correlation between length and stress is taken up in more detail in Chapters 4-6 (on phonology).

2.2.7 Diphthongs. All of the vowels described so far are MONOPHTHONGS, that is, vowel sounds produced with no significant movement of the tongue. For all intents and purposes, the tongue maintains the same position throughout the articulation of the vowel. German also has DIPH-THONGS, vowels produced by moving the tongue from one position to another (cf. Figure 2.6).

Figure 2.6 Tongue movement in the formation of diphthongs.

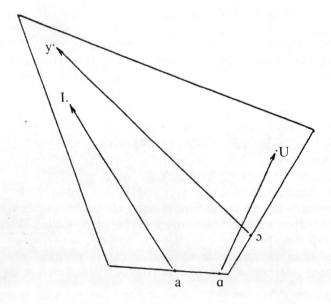

[aɪ]. This diphthong is heard initially in *Eile, Eis,* and *Eimer,* and finally in *Mai, sei,* and *Weih.* The tongue lies initially in the low-central position and is raised toward the [ɪ] position. In phonetic transcription, only the beginning and end points are noted. With the ear alone, i.e. without instrumentation, it is very difficult to ascertain just where the end point of the diphthong is. Hence, some pronouncing dictionaries transcribe this diphthong as [ae], and it is entirely possible that for many speakers this would represent a more accurate transcription. Note in Figure 2.5 the close proximity of [ɪ] and [e]. What is important in the articulation of the diphthong is that it ends in the 'neighborhood' of [ɪ]. That is the typical position, although some variation is possible without affecting the identification of it by the listener. The decision to use [aɪ] here rests on the results of recent experiments, which indicate that tongue-raising to [ɪ] is statistically most frequent.

Diphthongs are the result of a single articulatory movement of the tongue, and are approximately the same length as long vowels. And like long vowels they are heard as a single syllable. In our transcriptions, this fact needs to be accounted for, in order to distinguish the diphthong [aɪ] from the vowel sequence [a] + [ɪ], as in *algebraisch, archaisch, prosaisch,* etc. The diacritic mark '‿' is used under the second vowel, to indicate that it is not pronounced as a separate monophthong, hence, for example, [ʔaɪ] 'Ei'.

[aʊ]. This diphthong begins with the tongue somewhat further back than for [aɪ]. As the tongue is raised toward the [ʊ] position, the lips become rounded. The diphthong [aʊ] is heard initially in *auch, aus,* and *Auge,* medially in *kaum, Haus,* and '*raus,* and finally in *Sau, Frau,* and *lau.*

[ɔ̈]. The tongue assumes the position for [ɔ] and then moves toward the palate and tense [y] position. It is heard initially in *Eule, euch,* and *äußern,* medially in *neun, läuft,* and *Loipe,* and finally in *neu, heu,* and *Scheu.* Figure 2.6 charts the tongue movement for the three dipththongs just described.

Another set of diphthongs occurs with the 'reduced' vowel [ɐ], which is preceded by a 'full' vowel in the same syllable. As the second or nonsyllabic part of the diphthong, it will be marked with the diacritic '‿'. Table 2.4 inventories the possible combinations of 'full' vowel plus [ɐ].

Table 2.4 Diphthongs with [ɐ].

Bier [iːɐ]	Tür [yːɐ]	Uhr [uːɐ]
Hirt [ɪɐ]	mürbe [ʏɐ]	Furt [ʊɐ]
Meer [eːɐ]	Öhr [øːɐ]	Ohr [oːɐ]
Berg [ɛɐ]	Mörder [œɐ]	Mord [ɔɐ]
Mär [ɛːɐ]		
	Marsch [aɐ] Art [ɑːɐ]	

2.2.8 Nasalized vowels. In a relatively small number of words, most borrowed from the French, German has NASALIZED VOWELS, that is, vowels which are pronounced with the velum lowered, allowing air to escape through the nose (Figure 1.1). The vowels in *Teint* [ɛ̃:], *Bon* [ɔ̃:], and the final vowel in *Parfum* [œ̃:] and *Gourmand* [ã:] are all pronounced with the velum down. In phonetic transcription, the tilde (˜) is the usual symbol for nasalization.

All four of these vowels, which can also appear short when not stressed, can be replaced in speech by a combination of the short vowel plus the 'ng' sound, which is symbolized by [ŋ], i.e. [ɛŋ], [ɔŋ], [œŋ], and [aŋ]. This replacement varies as to speaker as well as with the individual word. *Teint*, for example, is pronounced almost exclusively with the nasalized vowel [ɛ̃:]. On the other hand, words ending orthographically in *-on*, e.g. *Balkon, Bonbon, Salon, Ballon*, etc., tend to have the pronunciation [ɔŋ] (even a third pronunciation is possible for *Balkon* and *Ballon:* [-o:n]). In general, one could say that the more frequently used words tend to be pronounced with vowel + [ŋ].

Problems (cf. Table 2.3).

Problem 1. Supply a phonetic symbol for each description given here. Indicate (with N/A) where a description does not apply to any German vowel.

    (1) low-central, short, unrounded vowel. . .
    (2) mid-central reduced vowel (schwa). . .
    (3) high-central, short, lax vowel. . .
    (4) high-back, tense, long rounded vowel. . .
    (5) mid-front, tense, long rounded vowel. . .
    (6) mid-front, lax, long unrounded vowel. . .
    (7) high-back, lax, short unrounded vowel. . .
    (8) high-front, lax, short unrounded vowel. . .
    (9) mid-front, lax, short unrounded vowel. . .
  (10) mid-front, lax, short rounded vowel. . .

Problem 2. Match the symbol with the appropriate description:

[e:] . . . (1) mid-back, lax, short rounded vowel
[y:] . . . (2) high-back, lax, short rounded vowel
[u] . . . (3) mid-front, lax, short rounded vowel
[o:] . . . (4) mid-back, tense, long rounded vowel
[ɑ:] . . . (5) high-front, lax, short rounded vowel
[ɛ] . . . (6) low-back, long unrounded vowel
[œ] . . . (7) mid-front, tense, long, unrounded vowel
[ɔ] . . . (8) high-front, tense, long, rounded vowel
[ʏ] . . . (9) mid-front, lax, short, unrounded vowel

Chapter 3
The consonant sounds
of German

3.0 Definition. In Chapter 2 consonants were defined provisionally as those sounds produced when the airstream from the lungs overcomes some impedence in the vocal tract. The present chapter outlines the details of consonant production. The discussion begins with a consideration of stops, which are produced by a complete closure in the vocal tract; then treats fricatives, characterized by a narrow aperture; and finally deals with nasals, trills, laterals, and onsets.

3.1 Stops

[p] [pʰ] [b] [b̥] **bilabial stops.** For the production of every sound in the language, muscular adjustments are made which result in particular acoustic impressions. Basically, the airstream pumped out by the lungs is modified in various ways and at various points along its path. If the airstream is momentarily blocked in the oral cavity, technically called OCCLUSION, the resulting sound is termed a STOP. Occlusion can be effected, for example, by closing the lips (as in the initial sound of *Post* or *Bus*), or by placing the blade of the tongue against the alveolar ridge (resulting in the initial sound of *Ton* or *dann*). There are at least five factors which play a role in determining the kind of stop produced: (1) the volume of air passing through the vocal tract; (2) the speed with which it traverses the vocal tract; (3) the speed with which the oral muscles contract to form the blockage or occlusion, and then relax, releasing the air; (4) where the occlusion occurs in the mouth; (5) the extent to which the vocal bands vibrate, and especially *when* they begin to vibrate.

The first three factors determine the degree of energy expended for the production of stops. A greater volume of air, i.e. higher air pressure and longer contraction time, results in a sound with a high energy component, e.g. the initial sound in **P**ost, **P**aß, **P**est, **P**orto. The two lips form the oc-

17

clusion (Figure 3.1) and the glottis is open (Figure 1.2a), i.e. the vocal cords are spread and hence not vibrating.

Figure 3.1 Position of the articulators for the bilabial stop (after Hans-Heinrich Wängler, *Instruction in German Pronunciation*, 3rd ed.; reproduced by permission of publisher).

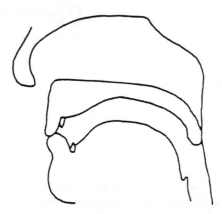

To describe the production of such a sound, a standard set of terms has been developed: 'stop', as noted, refers to the MANNER in which the airstream is modified. In the examples just given, the two lips are the articulators responsible for the closure, hence the stop is BILABIAL. The vocal bands do not vibrate, hence the sound is voiceless (unlike all the vowel sounds examined previously). And finally, there is a large volume of air passing through the vocal tract; the muscles of the lips are contracted fairly strongly. The term FORTIS (from the Latin, meaning 'strong') is used when referring to this sound. 'Voiceless' would also be appropriate, but as is seen later, all voiceless stops are not necessarily fortis, although the reverse is true.

The initial sound in **B**aß, **B**onn, **B**ug, and **b**in is likewise a bilabial stop. The lips form an occlusion, as illustrated in Figure 3.1. The volume of air is small and the muscles less active. It is termed a LENIS sound (from the Latin meaning 'weak'). The vocal cords may or may not vibrate. In some handbooks on German the sound is referred to simply as VOICED. Whereas it is useful for the foreign learner of German to learn initially that this sound is voiced, in actual speech situations one hears a voiceless sound more often than not. This question is taken up again later.

The articulation of the stop sounds can be broken down into three movements: (1) the creation of a closure; (2) occlusion, the period of closure itself (this may last from 60 to 150 milliseconds); (3) release. These movements are coordinated with other muscular activity in the vocal tract, such as the volume of air produced by the expiratory activity of the lungs and the opening and closing of the vocal cords. Hence, the TIM-

ING of these various movements with respect to one another is crucial in the production of sounds and the auditory impression they make on the listener.

In all the foregoing examples of bilabial stops, a vowel, i.e. a voiced sound, follows immediately upon the stop. The muscles of the vocal tract have to shift rapidly from one position to another. The initial sound in **Baß**, for example, is followed by a voiced sound. As soon as the lips are released (step (3)), the vowel sound is heard, i.e. release and voicing are simultaneous. In the case of the initial sound in **P***ost*, however, there is a delay in voicing. Voicing of the vowel does not begin simultaneously with the release of the lips. Rather, the airstream continues to pass through the oral tract for a brief period before voicing of the vowel begins. This delay in voicing is technically called ASPIRATION, and is often described as 'breathiness'. Its existence is easily illustrated by holding a piece of paper in front of the lips and pronouncing *Post*. The paper moves upon release of the lips, whereas for *Baß* there is no movement. The difference in timing is illustrated in Figure 3.2.

Figure 3.2 Timing in the articulation of stops. The horizontal straight line represents open glottis (voicelessness), the wavy line closed glottis (voicing). The point at which voicing begins is referred to as the 'Voice Onset Time'. Voicing begins after release in [pʰ], simultaneously with release in [p] and [b̥], and before release in [b] (after Ladefoged, *Preliminaries to Linguistic Phonetics;* reproduced by permission of the publisher).

Stop	Closure of the organs forming the occlusion Release of the organs forming the occlusion Onset of voicing
[pʰ]	aspiration vowel
[p][b̥]	vowel
[b]	vowel
Time	

In German, this difference in timing, resulting in aspiration, is one cue the listener has for distinguishing the fortis and lenis stops. The symbol [pʰ] is used here for the fortis aspirated bilabial stop, the raised 'h' indicating aspiration. The corresponding lenis is represented by [b] when the sound is voiced, by [b̥], with diacritic when it is unvoiced. Since most pronouncing dictionaries use [b] when the sound occurs initially, that practice is followed here, but only when referring to words articulated in isolation, e.g. *Bö* [bøː], *bei* [baɪ], *Bau* [baʊ]. Further discussion can be found in Chapter 6 on phonological rules and in Chapter 10 on sentence phonetics.

The aspirated stop [pʰ] is found at the beginning of stressed syllables, i.e. before that vowel which receives the greatest emphasis in a word. Hence, [pʰ] is found in *Appell, dupieren*, and *frappant* as well as initially in **P**ost, **P**est, **P**lan, and **P**racht. It also occurs at the end of words when they stand before a pause, as, for example, at the end of a sentence (*knapp, stop*, etc.). (In actual speech, degrees of aspiration occur. Such differences are ignored here, however, and the representation [pʰ] is adopted whenever a fortis bilabial stop occurs at the beginning of a syllable with a stressed vowel.)

We have referred to the 'paper test' in visually ascertaining the difference between [pʰ] and [b]. The paper moves when the initial sound in **P**aß is released. No movement takes place, however, when the bilabial stop in Spaß is released, nor in *spanne* (as compared with **P**anne) and *Spatzen* (as compared with **p**atzen). After the initial sound (written [ʃ] in the IPA), aspiration does not occur, i.e. the timing of the articulatory organs is identical to that of the lenis stop. Hence, aspiration occurs before stressed vowels only if the stop is not preceded by [ʃ]. This sound, a voiceless, unaspirated, bilabial stop, is symbolized by [p].

Before unstressed vowels, much less aspiration occurs than before stressed vowels. For the sake of simplicity of transcription, such degrees of aspiration are ignored here and fortis stops in that position are referred to simply as 'unaspirated', as, for example, in *Lappen, Lippe, Schuppen*, and *Raupen*.

In summary: [p] and [b] are both bilabial stops, sounds articulated by blocking the airstream momentarily at the lips and then releasing them. Bilabial stop [p] is fortis, [b] is lenis. The stop [pʰ] has the added feature of aspiration, which refers to the volume of air which continues flowing through the vocal tract after the release of closure, but before the onset of voicing of the following sound. [pʰ] occurs at the beginning of stressed syllables unless preceded by [ʃ], as in *Spaß*. Lenis stops may be either voiced ([b]) or voiceless ([b̥]).

[t] [tʰ] [d] [d̥] lamino-alveolar stops. Stop sounds can also be made by placing the tongue against the alveolar ridge. The tip of the tongue, the apex, and the area adjacent to it, the blade (or laminal area), is the ARTICULATOR (cf. Figure 1.4). The alveolar ridge is the POINT OF ARTICULATION. Such a stop can be described as LAMINOALVEOLAR[1] (cf. Figure 3.3). Exam-

---

1. Some accounts of German phonetics refer only to the apex, and call such a sound an 'apicoalveolar stop'. Since the tongue *may* touch the incisors as well, yet other descriptions use the term 'apicodental'.

ples in German of laminoalveolar stops are found initially in t*reu*, T*or*; d*u* and d*umpf.*

Figure 3.3 Position of the organs for the laminoalveolar stop (after Hans-Heinrich Wängler, *Instruction in German Pronunciation,* 3rd ed.; reproduced by permission of the publisher).

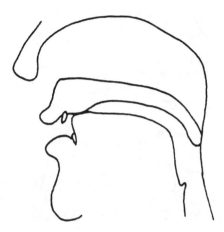

Much of what was said for the bilabial stops applies here as well voiceless, fortis stop is heard initially in T*on,* t*un,* and t*reu;* fi*nally in* ba*t,* and n*ett.* It is aspirated before a stressed vowel except af*ter [ʃ] as* st*ill,* St*adt,* and st*ur.* The aspirated stop is symbolized by [tʰ], t*he unaspir*ated by [t]. Thus, [tʰ] represents the boldface letter in T*est,* T*rick. Beta* and K*apitän,* i.e. at the head of a stressed syllable, [t] the soun*d in Stempe* and St*ück.* In final position, the aspirated sound occurs bef*ore a pause* otherwise the unaspirated [t] occurs.

A lenis stop is heard initially in d*umm* and d*reschen* ([d] or [*d̥] and me*dially in P*uder* and L*eder* ([d]). Again, the convention is adop*ted of using* [d] when discussing words spoken in isolation.

[k] [kʰ] [g] [g̊] dorsovelar stops. The broad, flat part of the tongue is called the DORSUM (cf. Figure 1.4). It can be raised in any number of places to make contact with the roof of the mouth, which can be divided roughly into the hard palate, the soft palate, and the uvula (Figure 1.1). The dorsum, on the other hand, has no distinct physiological boundaries. Phoneticians, however, often refer to the front part of the dorsum as PREDORSAL, and the back as POSTDORSAL. For simplicity of description, we simply use the term DORSO when labeling these sounds articulated with that part of the tongue which lies behind the blade (cf. Figure 1.4). When the postdorsal region is raised to form an occlusion with the velum, the resulting sound following the release is that heard initially in K*uh,* K*uß,* G*old,* and **Guß**. The articulator is the postdorsum, the point of articulation is the velum. Such stops, then, are DORSOVELAR (cf. Figure 3.4).

Figure 3.4 Position of the organs for the dorsovelar stops (after Hans-Heinrich Wängler, *Instruction in German Pronunciation*, 3rd ed.; reproduced by permission of the publisher).

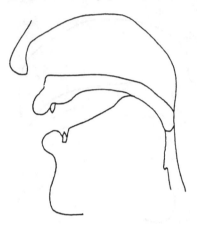

The initial sound in **K**uh, **K**uß, **K**ost, and **K**ot is fortis and aspirated, in IPA transcription represented by [kʰ]. The initial sound in **G**old, **G**uß, **g**urren, and **G**ott is lenis, represented by [g̊] (voiceless) and [g] (voiced). Again, [g] is used when treating words spoken in isolation. The unaspirated, fortis [k] occurs after [s] in *Skat* and *Skala* and when not occurring before a stressed vowel, as in *Backe, Laken, Fleck, Fanatiker*, and *Bäckerei*.

Most of these examples illustrate the dorsovelar stop before a back vowel. If you pronounce **Kuß** and then **Kies**, you can probably ascertain that the point of articulation for the two stops is not the same. The point for the initial sound in *Kies* is further forward. In fact, close observation reveals that a number of different contact points are made, depending on the vowel following. Try pronouncing *Kies, Käse, Kasse, Kuh*, and *Kost*. Several different points of articulation can be isolated. But in order to simplify the presentation, we work with the fiction of a single point of articulation, the dorsovelar position. Otherwise, our description would get lost in a mass of detail which would contribute little to an understanding of the German sound system.

The discussion of stops is summarized in Table 3.1. A certain amount of redundancy is evident, since fortis stops are always voiceless and lenis stops are never aspirated.

3.2 Fricatives. If, instead of closing off the pulmonary airstream entirely, the articulator is raised very close to the point of articulation, turbulence results. For example, the initial sound of **f**aul and **f**ast is formed by lightly placing the lower lip against the upper teeth and blowing the air be-

Table 3.1 Stops.

	Voice	Aspiration	Point of articulation: Bilabial	Lamino-alveolar	Dorso-velar
Fortis:	voiceless	unasp.	p	t	k
		asp.	pʰ	tʰ	kʰ
Lenis:	voiceless	...	b̥	d̥	g̊
	voiced	...	b	d	g

tween them. The noisiness of such sounds results from the air passing through the narrow slit or aperture formed by the teeth and lips. The air 'rubbing' against the confines of the slit gives this sound the name FRICATIVE. (Some handbooks use the term SPIRANT (from the Latin 'breath of air'); a few use CONSTRICTIVE, which, like 'stop', refers to the kind of resistance offered to the pulmonary airstream).

As with the stops, we proceed from the front of the mouth to the back.

[f] labiodental fortis fricative. As mentioned earlier, this fricative is produced when the upper incisors rest on the lower lip and air is blown through the narrow opening between them, e.g. initially in **f**aul, **f**ast, **F**ürst, and **Ph**ase. The articulator is the labium (lip), the place of articulation is the upper teeth; hence, it is a labiodental sound. The volume of air is large and the duration of the constriction relatively long; hence [f] is fortis (and like all fortis sounds, also voiceless).

[v] [v̥] labiodental lenis fricatives. The initial sound in **W**ein, **w**o, **w**issen, and **V**ase is likewise a labiodental fricative, the lenis counterpart of [f]. It is articulated with a smaller volume of air and less muscle contraction, which also renders the sound somewhat shorter than [f]. Lenis [v] is usually voiced in the pronunciation of isolated words. In normal, rapid speech, voicing may begin at various points during the formation of the constriction, or may not begin at all until the following vowel, parallel to the lenis stops. Should voice be absent entirely, the symbol [v̥] is used.

The difference between voiceless [f] and voiceless [v̥] can be illustrated by having a speaker of German contrast **F**all with **Qu**al and **F**ell with **Qu**elle. One notices that the initial [f] of **F**all and **F**ell is noisier than the fricative following initial [k] in **Qu**al and **Qu**elle, indicating greater turbulence of the air.

[s] laminoalveolar fortis fricative. When the surface of the tongue immediately behind the apex (the blade) is raised close to the alveolar ridge, a narrow aperture, or slit, is formed. The sides (lateral edges) of the tongue are pressed against the inner edges of the upper teeth. Without activating the vocal cords, the medial consonant in *wissen* and *reißen* is produced. The high degree of noisiness is enhanced by the airstream's passing over the edge of the teeth.

[z] [z̥] laminoalveolar lenis fricatives. The addition of voice to [s] results in the sound heard initially in *sich*, *Sohne* and *so*. As with other lenis consonants discussed earlier, the onset of voicing may occur at various times during the constriction, even to the extent that it is absent entirely, especially in initial position. In South Germany, Switzerland, and Austria, voiced [z] is virtually excluded from this position, even by speakers using the standard language, i.e. dialect-free speech. In transcribing words spoken in isolation, the symbol [z] is used. Without voicing, the lenis sound is symbolized with the usual diacritic: [z̥].

[ʃ] dorsoprepalatal fortis fricative. The initial sound of **sch**on, **sch**icken, and **Sch**uh is likewise characterized by a high degree of noisiness. It is fortis, i.e. a high air-flow sound. The front part of the tongue forms a constriction against the front part of the hard palate, resulting in a rill-shaped constriction. In addition, the lips are strongly rounded (cf. Figure 3.5).

Figure 3.5 Position of the organs for the articulation of [ʃ] (after Hans-Heinrich Wängler, *Instruction in German Pronunciation*, 3rd ed.; reproduced by permission of the publisher). (b) Shape of the aperture through which the air passes.

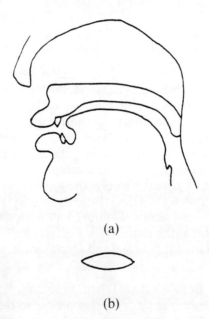

(a)

(b)

[ʒ] [ʒ̊] **dorsoprepalatal lenis fricatives.** The corresponding dorso-prepalatal lenis fricative occurs only in words borrowed into German from other languages, mainly from French and Italian. It is usually voiced, but some speakers in some words use a voiceless variety. Examples: *Etage, Ingenieur, Garage, Journal, Jalousie* (cf. Appendix 3).

[s][z][ʃ] and [ʒ] are sometimes referred to as 'sibilants'.

[ç] **dorsopalatal fortis fricative.** The final sound in *ich, euch, Milch, König,* and *Storch* is produced by raising the central area of the dorsum close to the hard palate to form a slit. The lips are spread. The sound is fortis (and, of course, voiceless). Cf. Figure 3.6.

Figure 3.6 Position of the organs for the articulation of [ç] and [j] (after Hans-Heinrich Wängler, *Instruction in German Pronunciation,* 3rd ed.; reproduced by permission of the publisher).

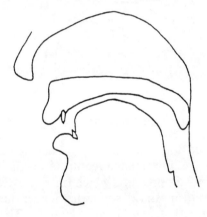

[j] [j̊] **dorsopalatal lenis fricatives.** The corresponding lenis fricative occurs initially in *ja, jung,* and *je.* Although lenis and voiced, it is articulated with somewhat more energy than the initial sound of English *yard* and *yes,* i.e. the constriction is narrower and the volume of air greater, but the turbulence is by no means as great as for [ç] (cf. Figure 3.6).

[x] **dorsovelar fortis fricative.** The fricative heard finally in *Buch, Fach, auch,* and *doch* is formed by placing the back part of the tongue, the postdorsal area, close to the velum (soft palate), and forcing the airstream through the resulting slit. The place of articulation may also occur somewhat further back, but for the sake of simplicity of description, this sound is referred to here as dorsovelar (cf. Figure 3.7).

[ɣ][ɣ̊] **dorsovelar lenis fricatives.** The lenis counterpart to fortis [x] is the sound frequently heard initially in *rühmen, rauchen, rot,* and *Rinne* in normal, rapid speech. In the careful pronunciation of isolated words, the initial sound of these words is rendered as a trill, the rapid vibration of one organ against another. But in rapid speech the initial sound in these words is likely to be a lenis fricative. It may also be articulated somewhat further back than [x], postvelar or uvular, for which the symbol is [ʁ]. But for purposes of descriptive simplicity, it is here treated as dorsovelar (cf. Figure 3.7).

> *Figure 3.7* Position of the organs for the articulation of [x] and [ɣ] (after Hans-Heinrich Wängler, *Instruction in German Pronunciation*, 3rd ed.; reproduced by permission of the publisher).

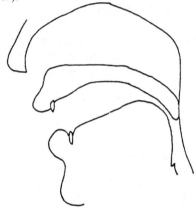

Summary. As with the stops, the terms 'fortis' and 'lenis' have been used as cover terms for several interrelated features. 'Fortis' encompasses (1) the phenomenon of high air pressure, which is manifested in fricatives as greater turbulence or noisiness; (2) somewhat longer duration caused by greater muscular contraction; and (3) voicelessness. The term 'fortis', of course, is relative and must be contrasted with 'lenis' for the terms 'longer', 'greater', and 'higher' to make sense. 'Lenis' refers to (1) lower air pressure, hence less pronounced turbulence in fricatives (for some, especially [v] and [j], the degree of 'frication' may be so low as to be virtually absent); and (2) shorter duration for the constriction. Voicing is not an essential feature of lenis fricatives. It is heard most often medially between vowels, since the vowels on either side are voiced, and the vocal bands usually continue to vibrate through the articulation of the consonant, as, for example, in *Löwe* [v], *Phase* [z], *Page* [ʒ], *Koje* [j], and *Meere* [ɣ]. Table 3.2 summarizes the inventory of fricative sounds.

3.3 The vowel onsets. The stop and fricative consonants are referred to collectively as OBSTRUENTS, sounds which offer resistance to the pulmonary airstream. Handbooks often include two other sounds under this heading: (1) the initial sound in *hin, her,* and *Haß;* (2) the 'glottal stop', the sharp onset of the initial vowel in, for example, *aus* and *und,* which is also heard in American English 'uh-uh' (= 'no').

Table 3.2 Fricatives.

Point of articulation:	Voice	Labio-dental	Lamino-alveolar	Dorso-prepalatal	Dorso-palatal	Dorso-velar	Uvular
Fortis:	vl	f	s	ʃ	ç	x	
Lenis:	vd	v	z	ʒ	j	ɣ	ʁ
	vl	v̥	z̦	ʒ̊	j̊	ɣ̊	

[h]. The initial sound of *hin, her,* and *Haß* is described variously as an ORAL-GUTTURAL fricative, a LARYNGEAL or LARYNGEAL-PHARYNGEAL fricative, or as a GLOTTAL fricative. The plethora of designations for the point of articulation is itself an indication that this sound does not lend itself to classification by the terms we have been using, terms which give (1) the articulating organ and (2) the organ against which it is articulated. When one pronounces slowly a series such as *hin, her, Haß, Hose, Huhn,* it is clear that the vocal tract assumes the position of the following vowel even before the initial [h] is pronounced. Thus there is no point of articulation in the sense in which we have been using it to describe the stops and fricatives. In a sense, there are as many '*h*-sounds' as there are vowels. We do not use a separate symbol for each, however, but employ the IPA symbol [h]. We call this sound a 'breathy onset', the term 'onset' being understood as a way of 'getting into' the following vowel. The amount of 'breathiness' is correlated with the height of the following vowel. The higher the vowel, the narrower the opening in the oral cavity and the more audible the friction. In rapid speech between vowels, it may be voiced, e.g. in *Uhu* and *Hoheit.*

[ʔ]. A second type of onset is referred to as a GLOTTAL STOP or GLOTTAL CATCH. It is articulated by drawing the vocal bands together along their entire length and then releasing them suddenly for the voiced articulation of the following vowel. It is the sudden release 'into' the vowel which creates the staccato impression in a phrase such as *ein altes Auto,* where the beginning of each word is initiated by a glottal stop.

Insofar as the glottal stop includes closure (of the vocal cords), occlusion, and release, the term 'stop' is understandable. However, it is not articulated in the oral cavity with an articulator and place of articulation. Furthermore, the terms 'fortis' and 'lenis' are inappropriate since they refer, in part, to the volume of air in the oral cavity. Both [h] and [ʔ] actually belong to the PHONATION PROCESS, not the articulatory process. Hence, they should not be classified with the obstruents, as happens in many handbooks on phonetics where such a classification rests more on their FUNCTIONAL aspect in languages (they behave like obstruents), rather than on their physical production.

As mentioned earlier, the glottal stop occurs with word-initial vowels, e.g. *arm* [ʔaɐ̯m], *elf* [ʔɛlf], *oft* [ʔɔft]. But it also tends to occur before any vowel-initial morpheme which carries some degree of stress, e.g. *Verein* [fɛɐ̯ʔaɪn], *be'enden* [bəʔɛndən], *'ur'alt* [ʔuːɐ̯ʔalt], etc., and even in the middle of a morpheme before a stressed vowel, e.g. *The'ater* [teʔaːtɐ]. To what extent the glottal stop accompanies such vowels depends on a number of linguistic and nonlinguistic factors which are not gone into here. For the purposes of this study, however, a glottal stop is transcribed whenever a vowel occurs at the beginning of a stressable morpheme, e.g. *aufesse* [ʔaʊfʔɛsə]. (Both *auf* and *esse* are 'stressable'; here *auf* has the PRIMARY STRESS (cf. Chapter 10 on stress.)

3.4 Nasals. The obstruents (stops and fricatives) are all articulated with the velum raised so that the airstream passes through the oral cavity (Figure 1.4). If the velum is lowered, the airstream can also pass through the nasal cavity (Figure 1.1). Sounds articulated with a lowered velum are called NASAL.

[m] bilabial nasal. The same articulators and points of articulation which were described for the stops are used for the articulation of the nasal sounds in German. For the initial sound in M*ann,* M*aus,* m*alen,* and m*ir,* the two lips form a closure. The sound differs from [b] in the fact that the velum is lowered and no air pressure builds up in the oral cavity, since the airstream flows through the nose. As with the other nasals in German, it is voiced, but, in our description of the nasals, the term 'voiced' can be omitted.

[n] lamino-alveolar nasal. With the laminal area of the tongue against the alveolar ridge, the same position as for [d], and with the velum lowered, the initial sound in n*a,* N*uß,* n*aß,* and n*iesen* is produced.

[ŋ] dorsovelar nasal. It was noted for the dorsovelar stops that the point of articulation was dependent on the accompanying vowel. This is also true for the corresponding nasal; again, here, just one position is chosen as representative of this nasal, which is articulated with the postdorsal area of the tongue against the lowered velum. It is heard finally in D*i*ng, *Erscheinu*ng, *la*ng, and *ju*ng; before [k] in *de*nk*en,* A*n*k*er,* and *He*nk*er,* before [s] in A*ng*st and *He*ng*st.*

3.5 The lateral [l]. The initial sound in L*eiter,* l*aden,* l*os,* and L*ust* is articulated with the laminal area of the tongue against the alveolar ridge, as for [t], [d], and [n]. The sides of the tongue (LATUS, cf. Figure 1.4) are drawn in away from the inner edge of the upper teeth, allowing the airstream to pass between the edge of the tongue and the teeth. (With the obstruents, the airstream is directed through the center of the oral cavity.) The vocal cords vibrate. The back of the tongue, the dorsum, is low, which accounts for the characteristic 'bright' sound of the German lateral. Failure to keep the dorsum low results in a so-called 'dark *l*' or velarized *l* which is foreign to standard German, but common in English (especially when the lateral occurs adjacent to a back vowel).

3.6 The trills [r],[R]. TRILLS in German are articulated in two ways: either the apex vibrates against the alveolar ridge ([r]), or the dorsum is raised close to the velum, the uvula then vibrating against the surface of the tongue ([R]); cf. Figure 3.8. Speakers of German generally use either

Figure 3.8 Position of the organs for the articulation of the uvular trill (top) and the apical trill (bottom) (after Hans-Heinrich Wängler, *Instruction in German Pronunciation,* 3rd ed.; reproduced by permission of the publisher).

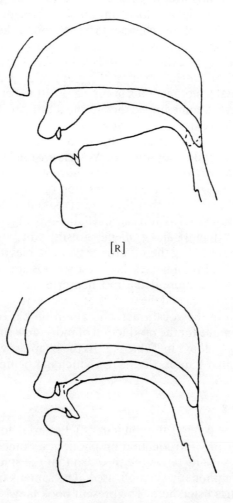

[R]

[r]

one or the other, not both interchangeably. In slow, careful speech or in isolated words, it is heard in initial position in such words as **R**u*hm*, *rennen*, **R***ing*, and **R***ost*, and before the vowel in *fahre, Meere, Marine,* and *größere.* In normal, rapid speech, trilling is less likely to occur. Often it is replaced in the contemporary language with [ɣ] (cf. under 'fricatives').

3.7 Consonantal sonorants. The nasals, lateral, and trills are grouped together by many linguists under the heading SONORANTS or CONSONANTAL SONORANTS. Like the obstruents, this class of sounds is characterized by some resistance to the pulmonary airstream: nasals have an occlusion in the oral cavity; laterals block the airstream from exiting through the center of the oral cavity; trills interrupt the airstream intermittently. On the other hand, there is no intraoral pressure build-up as with the stops. In the production of nasals, the air flows unimpeded through the nose; in the production of the lateral, the channel formed around the lateral edges of the tongue is wide enough to prevent audible friction; the interruption of the airstream in the production of trills is so brief as to prevent any significant build-up of air pressure behind the place of articulation.

The consonantal sonorants thus occupy a position between obstruents and vowels. There is some impedance to the airstream, less than for the obstruents, but more than for the vowels.

The degree of impedance to the airstream in these three major classes of sounds results in a gradient of sonority. Vowels are the most sonorous, the consonantal sonorants are the next most sonorous, and the obstruents are the least sonorous. The intermediate position of the consonantal sonorants is reflected in the fact that they are classified as 'consonants', yet they, like vowels, may act as SYLLABICS, syllable-bearing sounds, as, for example, in *Handel* [handl̩], and *großem* [gʀoːsm̩], where the final sound is responsible for our hearing these words as two syllables (the stroke underneath the [l] and the [m] indicates that these sounds are syllable-forming). They are discussed in more detail in Chapter 6.

This chapter has discussed the sounds of German from the viewpoint of their articulation in the vocal tract, and attention has been centered on the adjustments made for the production of individual sounds. A summary of our findings follows in Table 3.3. In the chapters which follow, the PATTERNS of German sounds, the SYSTEM which lies behind the sounds we hear, are discussed.

Further reading

There are three general pronouncing dictionaries for German, each prefaced by a lengthy introduction on phonetics. Some slight transcriptional differences characterize the three, so that the student should consult the tables on phonetic symbols used. The same is true for the other books of phonetics listed here. The present book largely follows the system employed in:

Table 3.3 The consonant sounds of German.

Articulation:		B	LD	LA	DPP	DP	DV	U	O
Obs.		vl vd	vl vd	vl vd	vl vd	vl vd	vl vd	vl vd	
	Stops: for.	pʰ p		tʰ t			kʰ k		
	len.	b̥ b		d̥ d			g̊ g		
	Fricatives: for.		f	s	ʃ	ç	x		
	len.		v̥ v	z̥ z	ʒ̊ ʒ	j̊ j	ɣ̊ ɣ	ʁ	
Son.	Nasals:	m		n			ŋ		
	Trills:			r				ʀ	
	Lateral:			l					
	Onsets:								h ʔ

Key: Obs., Obstruents
    Son., Sonorants
    for., fortis
    len., lenis
    vl., voiceless
    vd., voiced

B, bilabial
LD, labiodental
LA, laminoalveolar
DPP, dorsoprepalatal

DP, dorsopalatal
DV, dorsovelar
U, uvular
O, onset

Wörterbuch der deutschen Aussprache. 1969. 2. Aufl. München: Hueber. (First edition, Leipzig: VEB Enzyklopädie, 1964.)

The other two major dictionaries are:

Duden. 1974. Aussprachewörterbuch. 2. Aufl. Mannheim/Wien/Zürich: Dudenverlag (Der große Duden; Band 6).
Siebs. 1969. Deutsche Aussprache. 19. Aufl. Berlin: Walter de Gruyter & Co.

Books on German phonetics can be divided into those which treat orthoepy (correct pronunciation) and those whose purpose is to describe.

Orthoepical:

Kreuzer, Ursula u. Klaus Pawlowski. 1971. Deutsche Hochlautung. Praktische Aussprachelehre. (With tapes.) Stuttgart: Klett.
Martens, Carl. 1966. Abbildungen zu den deutschen Lauten. 2. Aufl. München: Hueber.
MacCarthy, Peter. 1975. Pronunciation of German. London: Oxford University Press.
Stötzer, Ursula. 1975. Deutsche Aussprache. (With two records.) Leipzig: VEB Verlag Enzyklopädie.
Wängler, Hans-Heinrich. 1974. Grundriß einer Phonetik des Deutschen. 3. Aufl. Marburg: Elwert.

_____. 1972. Instruction in German pronunciation. 3rd ed. St. Paul: EMC Corp.

Descriptive:

Kohler, Klaus J. 1977. Einführung in die Phonetik des Deutschen. Berlin: Schmidt.

German phonetics contrasted with English is represented by:

Moulton, William G. 1962. The sounds of English and German. Chicago: University of Chicago Press.

Recent books and articles on German phonetics can be located in *Germanistik;* studies prior to 1971 are indexed in *Bibliographie zur Phonetik und Phonologie des Deutschen* (Institut fur Phonetik der Universität Köln), Tübingen: Niemeyer, 1971.

A number of works on general phonetics are available. Perhaps the best conceived with the beginning student in mind is:

Ladefoged, Peter. 1982. A course in phonetics. 2nd ed. (First edition, 1975.) New York: Harcourt Brace Jovanovich.

For a very extensive overview of all areas of phonetics:

Borden, Gloria J., and Katherine S. Harris. 1980. Speech science primer. Physiology, acoustics and perception of speech. London and Baltimore: William & Wilkins.

Problems (cf. Table 3.3).

Problem 1. Supply a phonetic symbol for each description given.
 (1) Laminoalveolar, fortis, aspirated stop . . .
 (2) Uvular trill . . .
 (3) Laminoalveolar nasal . . .
 (4) Labiodental voiced fricative . . .
 (5) Dorsovelar fortis fricative . . .
 (6) Dorsopalatal lenis voiceless fricative . . .
 (7) Dorsoprepalatal fortis fricative . . .
 (8) Bilabial nasal . . .
 (9) Glottal stop . . .
(10) Laminoalveolar, lenis voiced stop . . .
(11) Dorsovelar, fortis aspirated stop . . .
(12) Dorsoprepalatal lenis, voiced fricative . . .
(13) Dorsovelar, lenis voiced fricative . . .

Problem 2. Give the linguistic descriptions for each of the following symbols.
 (1) [g] . . .
 (2) [ʃ] . . .

(3) [l] ...
(4) [r] ...
(5) [x] ...
(6) [d] ...
(7) [ç] ...
(8) [ŋ] ...
(9) [z] ...
(10) [tʰ] ...
(11) [p] ...
(12) [ɣ] ...

Problem 3. Give the phonetic description for the fricatives in the following phonetic transcriptions:

(1) Gras   [gɣɑːs] ...
            ...
(2) fesch   [fɛʃ]   ...
            ...
(3) weiß   [vaɪs]   ...
            ...
(4) acht   [ʔaxt]   ...
            ...
(5) Pech   [pʰɛç]   ...
            ...
(6) Page   [pʰɑːʒə] ...

Problem 4. Which of the following transcriptions with voiceless stops should be supplied with the symbol for aspiration? Add the raised 'h' symbol where appropriate. The raised perpendicular line in the transcription indicates that the following syllable is stressed.

(1) Tresor [t ɣeˈzoːɐ̯]
(2) König [k øːnɪç]
(3) zeitig [tsaɪt ɪç]
(4) Vater [faːt ɐ]
(5) lapidar [lap iˈdaːɐ̯]
(6) Konsonant [k ɔnzoˈnant]
(7) akustisch [ʔaˈk uːst ɪʃ]
(8) Pille [p ɪlə]
(9) fatal [faˈt aːl]
(10) Tapet [t aˈp eːt]
(11) notiert [noˈt iːɐ̯t]
(12) tolerant [t oleˈɣant]
(13) akut [ʔaˈk uːt]
(14) direkt [diˈɣɛk t]

Chapter 4
Phonology: The inventory
of phonemes

4.0 A second perspective on sounds: Different versus distinctive. In the
previous two chapters sounds were considered from the point of view of
their articulation, the adjustments various organs make in modifying the
pulmonary airstream. Our phonetic transcriptions represent TYPICAL pro-
ductions of sounds, since it is an experimental fact that no two sounds are
exactly alike. The very fact that we speak about the typical production of a
sound already presupposes that numerous different physical events are
considered by speaker and hearer to be equivalent. For example, the word
Ei can be pronounced by different speakers at different speeds, sometimes with glottal stop [ʔaɪ], sometimes without [aɪ], sometimes with a
slightly lower vowel [ae̞], [ʔae̞], etc. Yet the native speaker hears all of
these different renderings of the word *Ei* as the same in spite of the experimental evidence to the contrary (no two sounds are exactly the same). A
number of hypotheses could be proposed to try to explain the discrepancy
between empirical evidence and the judgments of the native speakers of
the language. (1) The listeners relate them all to the same meaning; after
all, [ʔaɪ], [aɪ], [ae̞], [ʔae̞], etc. must all mean 'egg'. There are no other possibilities for interpreting these utterances. (2) The physical differences between [ʔaɪ], [aɪ], [ae̞], [ʔae̞], for example, are not great enough to allow any
other interpretation than that they are basically the same. (3) Listeners
are simply not able to hear such minute differences. (4) Our human perceptual apparatus groups together different physical signals as if they
were one. (5) They are all related to the same spelling.

The last hypothesis can be discarded immediately, since we are concerned at this point only with the spoken language. Illiterates make the
same judgments here as literate speakers. Furthermore, the phenomenon
is observable for every language, whether the speakers are literate or not.

Hypothesis (1) focuses on meaning, and is actually not separable from (2). There is some range of 'tolerance' regarding the way a word can be pronounced and still have it identifiable as 'the same word'. But a great deal of experimental evidence would be needed before one could say just what the bounds of tolerance are. It may or may not be the case that small differences cannot be heard by the untrained listener (hypothesis (3)). In the case in question, listeners have simply learned to ignore any differences.

Hypothesis (4) is similar to (2). It recognizes that our perceptions are discrete, that is, they IMPOSE structure on stimuli, whether these be visual or aural. The different auditory stimuli, symbolized earlier by using different phonetic transcriptions, constitute a single entity for the speakers of German; this entity is commonly called the PHONEME.

Chapters 2 and 3 were concerned with describing a fairly large number of sounds *qua* sounds. In this chapter we are interested in which sounds native speakers of German judge to be the 'same', and which 'different', irrespective of how many sounds the professional phonetician can isolate.

This twofold perspective on the study of sounds can be illustrated with an analogy. At one time or another you may have heard Simon and Garfunkel's 'The Sounds of Silence', sometimes sung, sometimes performed solely with instruments. In both instances you were able to identify what you heard as being the same song, even though in some respects the performances were quite different—one vocal, one solely instrumental. The reason is, of course, simple: the same score underlies both performances. The score is, as it were, the abstract representation which has to underlie every performance of 'The Sounds of Silence' for it to be recognized as such. This analogy can be applied to the study of sounds: phonology is the abstract score ('abstract' because it is not audible) and phonetics is the performance of the score.

The study of sounds in language:	
Phonetics:	Phonology:
Physical events,	Abstract,
Audible 'performances'	'The score'

We have said that phonology is interested in the question as to which sounds the native speakers of a particular language judge to be the same, and which are judged to be different. Two examples illustrate this point. Suppose we hear two sentences of German, which we transcribe phonetically as follows:

[vil zi: ʀaɪs] (Will sie Reis?)
[vil zi: ɣaɪs] (Will sie Reis?)

Let us assume that the only difference comes at the beginning of the last word: [ʀ] versus [ɣ], a uvular trill versus a voiced dorsovelar fricative. There is no question that the two sounds are different. One, in fact, is classified as a consonantal sonorant, the other as a fricative within the larger class of obstruents. The two sounds are different physically. Yet the native speaker-hearer adjudges them the same. The reason is that the physical DIFFERENCE does not contribute to DISTINGUISHING two different meanings; [ʀaɪs] and [ɣaɪs] are identified as having the same semantics, that is, as the same word. The difference between [ʀ] and [ɣ] is not distinctive, that is, it is not the sort of physical difference which matters to a native speaker of German. The sounds are different on the phonetic level, but they are not distinctive on the phonemic level, where 'distinctive' is defined as those phonetic features which function in the language to signal different meanings.

The second case uses the following two examples.

[vɪl zi: ʀaɪs]   (Will sie Reis?)
[vɪl zi: maɪs]   (Will sie Mais?)

Here again, in a comparison of the two utterances, there is a difference at one point. But this time the phonetic DIFFERENCE [ʀ] versus [m] is also DISTINCTIVE. The difference signals a difference in meaning. The two sounds can then be said to function as PHONEMES.

These, then, are the two constantly recurring cases in an examination of the sounds of any language. Some sounds get grouped together as one, e.g. [ʀ] and [ɣ]; they are different, but not distinctive. Others are both different and distinctive, e.g. [ʀ] and [m]. In this chapter, the sounds discussed in Chapters 2 and 3 are examined in order to ascertain what the distinctive differences are in German.

4.1 Minimal pairs. One traditional method of ascertaining the distinctive differences in languages has been the method of minimal pairs, also known as the commutation test. As in the example just given, *Reis* versus *Mais*, pairs of words are chosen which differ from one another at only one point. If the phonetic difference results in a meaning difference, then the two sounds are distinctive and are classified as phonemes.

In the same example, the two words compared occurred in sentences. Most linguists do not find it necessary always to find a context for the words compared. That is, pairs such as *Ruß* and *muß*, *Rain* and *mein*, could just as well show that the initial consonants are distinctive, even though they could hardly appear in the same position in the sentence due to their different word classes. Some linguists, however, feel that the notion of distinctive sound difference only makes sense if it is actually possible to show that in the same context, two sounds function to keep two distinct meanings apart. For German, either procedure leads to the same results. In the interest of space we compare individual words, most of which, however, could appear in the same context in a sentence, as do *Reis* and *Mais*.

4.2 The consonants. We begin systematically with the stop consonants, then take up the fricatives, the consonantal sonorants, and finally, the vowels.

4.2.1 The stops. Pairs such as *Paß-Baß, pellen-bellen,* and *Gepäck-Gebäck*, are all minimal pairs, since each differs at one and the same point, initially in: [pʰas]:[bas], [pʰɛlən]:[bɛlən], etc. and medially in: [gəpʰɛk]:[gəbɛk]. One can say, then, that the fortis bilabial stop and the lenis bilabial stop are phonemes because they CONTRAST with one another in the identical phonetic environment.

A contrast also occurs in the following pairs.

Staupe [ʃtaʊpə]   Staube [ʃtaʊbə]
schuppe [ʃupə]   schubbe [ʃubə]
Oper [ʔoːpɐ]   Ober [ʔoːbɐ]

Here again, fortis and lenis bilabial stops contrast. The only difference from the previous three examples is that the fortis stop is unaspirated.

The question arises, then, whether contrasts can now be found between the aspirated ([pʰ]) and the unaspirated ([p]) fortis stops. Again, one has to look for minimal pairs, but these simply do not occur. The reason can be found by examining Table 4.1, which shows that [pʰ] and [p] turn up in mutually exclusive environments. Fortis stops are aspirated at the beginning of stressed syllables (as long as they are not preceded by [ʃ], and when

Table 4.1 Aspiration and nonaspiration on the fortis stop /p/. The same distribution of aspirated and nonaspirated stops holds for all voiceless stop phonemes.

Phonetic environment:	Aspirated [pʰ]	Unaspirated [p]	Examples:	
(1) Beginning of a stressed syllable:	yes	yes	Panne	Spanne
With preceding /ʃ/ (or /s/):	no	yes	. . .	Spanne
(2) Before pause:	yes	no	Stopp!	. . .
(3) Beginning of an un-stressed syllable:	no	yes	. . .	separát
(4) End of a syllable:			. . .	Doppel

they occur before pause. Otherwise they are unaspirated. This means that we are never able to find minimal pairs, since minimal pairs depend on two given sounds occurring in the identical environment. When two sounds which otherwise share all other characteristics or features (here voicelessness, fortis, and stop articulation) appear in mutually exclusive phonetic environments, then they are simply variants or ALLOPHONES of one phoneme.

Thus [pʰ] and [p] are allophones of the phoneme /p/ (the phoneme is symbolized by placing the simpler of the two symbols between slashes). Returning to our earlier analogy: /p/ is the 'score', the allophones [pʰ] and [p] represent the 'performances' (the actual audible sounds). The performance differs depending on where /p/ occurs: [pʰ] at the beginning of stressed syllables (providing an obstruent does not precede) and before pause; [p] everywhere else.

To summarize: [pʰ] and [p] both contrast with [b], that is, minimal pairs can be found in both instances. But [pʰ] and [p] never contrast with each other. There are no minimal pairs. And since [pʰ] and [p] share all phonetic features but aspiration, they can be grouped together as members or allophones of the same abstract linguistic unit we have been calling the phoneme. A further indication that this is the correct analysis is evident when the same phoneme /p/ in a given word is phonetically aspirated in one environment, but not in another, for example, stopp! [ʃtɔpʰ] before pause, but stoppen [ʃtɔpn̩] elsewhere.

The same line of argumentation can be used in examining the lenis bilabial stops, symbolized in Chapter 3 as [b] and [b̥]. Table 4.2 shows that [b] and [b̥] must be allophones of one phoneme, symbolized /b/. In medial position, e.g. in leben, haben, and sieben, the phoneme is voiced: [b]. In initial position it is also voiced following a pause, or if the sound immedi-

Table 4.2 The distribution of the lenis allophones [b] and [b̥]. The same distribution holds for all lenis stop phonemes.

Phonetic environment:	Voiced [b]	Voiceless [b̥]	Examples:
(1) Medial position:			leben ...
(2) Initial position (a) after pause: (b) following a voiced sound:	yes	no	//Berge ... die Berge ...
(3) Following a voiceless sound:	no	yes	... das Boot

ately preceding it in the sentence is voiced (more on this in Chapter 11). Otherwise, /b/ is 'realized' as the voiceless [b̥], for example, in *des* B*ruders,* *Tischb*ein, etc.

In Chapter 3, we isolated the following sounds at the alveolar position (cf. Figure 3.3): [tʰ], [t], [d], and [d̥]. Parallel to the analysis of the bilabial stops, one can find minimal pairs when fortis and lenis stops are compared:

Tank [tʰaŋk]	Dank [daŋk] (or [d̥aŋk])
Teich [tʰaɪç]	Deich [daɪç] (or [d̥aɪç])
Puter [pʰuːtɐ]	Puder [pʰuːdɐ]
Seite [zaɪtə]	Seide [zaɪdə]

Fortis and lenis stops contrast with each other in the same phonetic environment, initially as well as medially, following the same pattern as was observed for /p/ and /b/. As with the bilabial stops, no contrast can be found between the unaspirated and the aspirated stops, nor between the voiced and voiceless lenis stops. The phoneme /t/, then, has two variants or allophones, [tʰ] and [t]; the phoneme /d/ has as allophones [d] and [d̥]. The distribution of the allophones parallels that given in Tables 4.1 and 4.2.

At the dorsovelar position, where [kʰ], [k], [g], and [g̥] occur, once again a contrast can be found between the fortis and lenis stops:

Kasse [kʰasə]	Gasse [gasə] (or [g̥asə])
Kunst [kʰʊnst]	Gunst [gʊnst] (or [g̥ʊnst])
Ecke [ʔɛkə]	Egge [ʔɛgə]
locke [lɔkə]	logge [lɔgə]

The distribution of allophones is the same as sketched in Table 4.1. The /k/ in K*ater,* K*ost,* and ma*k*ieren is aspirated; that in S*k*at, S*k*la*ve* (environment 1 in Table 4.1), B*äcker* (environment 3), M*akler* (environment 3), and T*rock*ner (environment 4) are unaspirated. The phonemes so far are as follows:

		labial	alveolar	velar
Stops:	fortis:	/p/	/t/	/k/
	lenis:	/b/	/d/	/g/

'Phoneme', as the term has been used thus far, is defined in two ways: (1) in terms of its phonetic content, the concrete sounds it represents, e.g. /p/ represents all fortis bilabial stops; and (2) in terms of its function as a contrastive unit; /p/, for example, contrasts with /b/, or more generally /p t k/ contrast with /b d g/ as fortis versus lenis. And the pairs /p b/, /t d/, and /k g/ contrast with each other in terms of the point of articulation.

4.2.2 The fricatives. We can follow the same procedure of looking for minimal pairs for the fricatives. In Chapter 3, the following systematic phones were isolated.

	Labio-dental	Lamino-alveolar	Dorso-prepalatal	Dorso-palatal	Dorso-velar
Fortis:	f	s	ʃ	ç	x
Lenis: voiced:	v	z	3	j̬	ɣ
voiceless:	v̥	z̥	3̥	j̊	ɣ̊

/f/ **vs.** /v/. Minimal pairs can be found for the labiodental fricatives, e.g.:

falten [faltn̩]	walten [valtn̩].
Felder [fɛldɐ]	Wälder [vɛldɐ]
feilen [faɪln̩]	weilen [vaɪln̩]
fälschen [fɛlʃn̩]	welschen [vɛlʃn̩]

No contrasts can be found in medial position due to the low incidence of [v] there. The same distribution of allophones observed for the lenis stops is true for the lenis fricatives as well: [v] occurs medially, e.g. in *Löwe, Möwe, hieven,* after pause and when the preceding sound in the sentence is voiced; [v̥] occurs otherwise. And since these two sounds occur in mutually exclusive environments (COMPLEMENTARY DISTRIBUTION is the term often used), they are allophones of one phoneme /v/. Thus /f/ and /v/ are contrastive units or phonemes at the labiodental position.

/s/ **vs.** /z/. The fricatives are not as widely distributed through the lexicon of German as are the stops. For this reason fewer minimal pairs are found, but still enough to show that fortis and lenis fricatives contrast. At the alveolar position:

/s/	/z/
reißen [ʀaɪsn̩]	reisen [ʀaɪzn̩]
Geißel [gaɪsl̩]	Geisel [gaɪzl̩]
weiße [vaɪsə]	weise [vaɪzə]
heißer [haɪsɐ]	heiser [haɪzɐ]

/ʃ/ **vs.** /3/. In Chapter 3 it was seen that [3] occurs only in words of foreign origin, and is relatively infrequent in German (some speakers, in fact, substitute [ʃ] for it in certain words, e.g. *Garage* and *Engagement*). With effort, a minimal pair or two can be found, e.g. *Marschen* [maʀʃn̩] 'marshlands' versus *Margen* [maʀ3n̩] 'margins' (of profit), but clearly [3] does not 'fit' well into the network of contrasts set up so far. It is not an allophone of [ʃ], since [3] neither has a predictable position in the word (as, say, aspirated stops do) nor does it occur in free variation with [ʃ] analogous to the behavior of [ɣ] and [ʀ]. Some analysts refer to it as a 'peripheral' or 'marginal' phoneme because of its ill fit. But since it does not behave like an allophone, and since minimal pairs are theoretically possible, it is here considered to be a phoneme of German.

/j/. Since [ç] rarely occurs word-initially and [j] occurs mainly initially, it is not possible to find contrastive pairs at the dorsopalatal position. But [j] is clearly a phoneme, since contrasts can be found with fricatives at other positions.

/z/	sage [zɑːgə]		/j/	jage [jɑːgə]
	säte [zɛːtə]			jäte [jɛːtə]
/ʃ/	Schar [ʃɑːʁ]			Jahr [jɑːʁ]
/f/	faucht [faʊ̯xt]			jaucht [jaʊ̯xt]

/x/. The two fricatives [ç] and [x] have an interesting distribution, as a comparison of the following word-pairs shows.

[ç]	[x]
Bücher	Buch
Süchte	Sucht
höchst	hoch
möchte	mochte
Mächte	Macht
Bäuche	Bauch

A comparison of the two columns shows that the two sounds alternate in the same morpheme.[1] They also occur in morphemes which have no alternates:

[ç]	[x]
ich	suchen
Pech	Bucht
Milch	doch
Mönch	lachen
Storch	auch

There are no minimal pairs in this list. The reason is clear: where [ç] occurs, [x] does not, and vice-versa. When one examines what sounds precede, the following distribution is noted.

---

1. A morpheme is the minimal form in a language to which a meaning can be assigned (or a grammatical function). *Buch* is a morpheme since it cannot be analyzed into smaller meaningful units. *Bücher* consists of two morphemes: *Buch* plus the plural marker, which consists of −*er* plus the fronting of the vowel. Morphology is the study of the forms of a language.

			Examples:	
i:	y:		siech	Tücher
I	Y		ich	Sprüche
e:	ø:	before [ç]	. . .	höchst
ɛ	œ		echt	möchte
	ɔy			euch
	aɪ			Eiche
consonants			manch Kelch durch	

		Examples:
u:		Buch
ʊ		Bucht
o:		hoch
ɔ	before [x]	Loch
a ɑ:		Dach brach
ɑʊ		tauchen

The fricative [ç] occurs after front vowels and consonants, [x] occurs after back vowels and [a]. The diphthong [ɔ̈] is 'fronting', that is, the tongue moves from back to front, front being the position before the articulation of [ç]; [aʊ] is a 'backing' diphthong. Since there is no overlap in their distribution, there can be no minimal pairs. The alternation is regular and predictable in the same way that aspirated and unaspirated fortis stops are. The fricative [x] occurs after back vowels and [a], [ç] occurs everywhere else. There is, then, one phoneme with two allophones which are in complementary distribution, or: the phoneme /x/ has two allophones: [x] after nonfront vowels, [ç] elsewhere.

In Chapter 3, two fricatives at the dorsovelar position were isolated: [x] and [ɣ]. Some minimal pairs can be found, such as *Wacht* [vɑxt] and *Wart* [vɑɣt], and *Bachen* [bɑxən] and *Barren* [bɑɣən]. It was also seen earlier in this chapter that [ɣ] and [ʀ] are simply variants of one phoneme. Either one could occur in the foregoing words. For reasons which become clear in Chapter 6, [ɣ] is treated as a variant of the phoneme /r/. (cf. 4.2.5).

4.2.3 The onsets [h] and [ʔ]. In Chapter 1, [h] and [ʔ] were termed 'onsets'. It might seem at first glance that these, too, form a contrast in German, since pairs of words, such as the following, occur.

heilen [haɪlən]	eilen [ʔaɪlən]
Hachse	Achse
Halm	Alm
Hast	Ast
Hecke	Ecke

But the fact that the glottal stop does not always occur speaks against its inclusion as a phoneme in German. In certain phonetic environments— for example, following a voiced sound—it is usually not produced. And its omission does not change the meaning of the word, as would be the case were [h] deleted.

The onset [h] usually occurs initially. Minimal pairs can be found with stops and fricatives.

/f/	fauchen	/h/	hauchen
	Fülle		Hülle
/z/	Sühne		Hüne
/v/	weben		heben
/ʃ/	Schein		Hain

The examples show that /h/ functions like any obstruent, and it is for this reason that many phoneticians classify it as a consonant. As was seen earlier, this classification cannot be justified on phonetic grounds. The phonemes so far are as follows.

		labial	alveolar	prepalatal	palatal	velar
Stops:	fortis	/p/	/t/			/k/
	lenis	/b/	/d/			/g/
Fricatives:	fortis	/f/	/s/	/ʃ/		/x/
	lenis	/v/	/z/	/ʒ/	/j/	
Onset						/h/

4.2.4 The nasals. The nasal phones [m], [n], and [ŋ] differ from one another in place of articulation. Minimal pairs are numerous. The nasal [ŋ], as noted earlier, has a rather restricted distribution. It occurs only after lax vowels, and appears in the same morpheme only before [s] and [k], e.g. *Angst* and *sinken*. In a few foreign words it occurs at a syllable boundary before [g] plus vowel, e.g. *Tango* and *Kongo*. Note the following minimal pairs.

/m/	/n/	/ŋ/
Macht	Nacht	. . .
kämmen	kennen	. . .
. . .	Tann	Tang
. . .	bannen	bangen
klimmen	. . .	klingen

4.2.5. The liquids /l/ and /r/. There is only one lateral [l] in German but it clearly has phonemic status, since it is commutatable with a number of other phonemes. For the commutation test other alveolar consonants are used.

/t/	Ton	/l/	Lohn
/d/	decken		lecken
/z/	Sehne		Lehne
/s/	heißen		heilen

/r/ is a phoneme as well, since minimal pairs can be found.

/l/ Lache	/r/ Rache
lau	rauh
Schlot	Schrot
fühlen	führen

We classify /r/ as a trill. Its various manifestations—alveolar trill [r], uvular trill [ʀ], velar fricative [ɣ], uvular fricative [ʁ] and mid-central vowel [ɐ]—are treated in Chapter 6.

Table 4.3 gives the inventory of consonantal phonemes set up for Modern Standard German. The notation for the place of articulation has been simplified.

Table 4.3 The consonant phonemes of Modern Standard German.

Point of articulation:		Labial	Alveolar	Pre-palatal	Palatal	Velar
Stops:	fortis	/p/	/t/			/k/
	lenis	/b/	/d/			/g/
Frica-	fortis	/f/	/s/	/ʃ/		/x/
tives:	lenis	/v/	/z/	/ʒ/	/j/	
Nasals:		/m/	/n/			/ŋ/
Lateral:			/l/			
Trill:			/r/			
Onset:						/h/

4.3 The vowels. The method of minimal pairs (the commutation test) can initially be applied to those vowels which were distinguished earlier in terms of tenseness and length.

[i:]	[I]	[y:]	[ʏ]
Miene	Minne	fühlen	füllen
siezen	sitzen	Fühler	Füller
Miete	Mitte	Hüte	Hütte

[e:]	[ɛ]	[u:]	[ʊ]
Beet	Bett	Ruhm	Rum
fehlen	fällen	spuken	spucken
schwelen	schwellen	Mus	muß

[ø:]	[œ]	[o:]	[ɔ]
Höhle	Hölle	Tone	Tonne
Röslein	Rößlein	Schote	Schotte
Schöße	schösse	Schrot	Schrott

The tense vowels also form oppositions among themselves, as do the lax vowels.

[i:]	[y:]	[u:]
Biene	Bühne	Buhne
spielen	spülen	spulen
Tier	Tür	Tour

[e:]	[ø:]	[o:]
	Getöse	Getose
lesen	lösen	losen
verheeren	verhören	
	Öde	Ode
Rebe		Robe

[ɪ]	[ʏ]	[ʊ]
Kippe		Kuppe
	Müll	Mull
	drücken	drucken
Sippe		Suppe
mißte	müßte	mußte

[ɛ]	[œ]	[ɔ]
	rösten	rosten
	dörren	dorren
Bäckchen	Böckchen	
kennten	könnten	konnten
Pest		Post

These 12 contrasting oppositions are distinguished by the phonetic features of (1) tense vs. lax, and (2) long vs. short.

If [ɛ:] is part of the standard language, and we assume that it is, minimal pairs can be found, for example, with short, lax [ɛ] and tense [e:].

/ɛ/	/ɛ:/	/e:/
stellen	stählen	stehlen
trennen	tränen	
	Mär	Meer
	Schären	Scheren

The two low vowels, [a] and [ɑ:], also contrast with each other.

/a/	/ɑ:/
Stadt	Staat
As	Aas
Massen	Maßen
bannen	bahnen
Schall	Schal

[ə]. Schwa is unique in that it occurs only in unstressed syllables. For that reason, minimal pairs are somewhat more difficult to find. Some examples:

Polo [pʰoːloˑ][2]	Pole [pʰoːlə]
Studentin [ʃtudɛntɪn]	Studenten [ʃtudɛntən]
Toto [tʰoːtoˑ]	Tote [tʰoːtə]
blanko [blaŋkoˑ]	blanke [blaŋkə]
Folio [foːli̯oˑ]	Folie [foːli̯ə]
Visa [viːzɑˑ]	Wiese [viːzə]

[ɐ]. Apparent minimal pairs with [ə] can be found, such as *Größe:größer* [gʀøːsə]:[gʀøːsɐ], but closer investigation shows that [ɐ] often alternates with [−əʀ] (or [−əɣ]) in the same morpheme, e.g. (1) in the comparative −*er: größer* [gʀøːsɐ] vs. *größere* [gʀøːsəʀə]; (2) in the agent suffix −*er: Lehrer* [leːʀɐ] vs. *Lehrerin* [leːʀəʀɪn]; (3) −*er* at the end of a lexical morpheme: *Hammer* [hamɐ] vs. *hämmere* [hɛməʀə]. In all these instances, [ɐ] and [əʀ−] alternate. There are two different pronunciations of the same morpheme. Whether [ɐ] or [əʀ−] (or [əɣ−]) appears, depends on the surrounding environment: [əʀ] occurs before vowels, [ɐ] otherwise. To look solely at pairs such as *Größe* with final [ə] and *größer* with final [ɐ] is misleading.

When the larger picture is observed, [ɐ] turns out to be one possible 'expression' of a single morpheme, the other being [əʀ] (or [əɣ]). How should this morpheme be represented phonemically? Surely not as both /ɐ/ and /ər/, since this would obscure the fact (which the spelling system recognizes) that no matter how it is pronounced, it is one and the same morpheme. Since that is the case, it should have a single representation. Which of the two possibilities should we choose? If /ɐ/, then we need to state that before a vowel it is realized as [əʀ] (or [əɣ]); if /ər/, then it must be stated that it is realized phonetically as [ɐ] when not occurring before a vowel. The latter is the preferred solution, since /ə/ and /r/ have already been established as phonemes. Nothing is gained in explaining how the phonological system of German is organized by assuming yet another phoneme.

Again it must be emphasized that the technique of minimal pairs is designed only to separate phonetic material. There is no principle of linguistic analysis which dictates that the analysis must remain on one 'level' (say the level of phonetics) if information from other 'levels' (say morphology) provides insight into the structure of the phonology. When we recognize that the same morpheme is involved (cf. the foregoing examples), then this fact should have a place somewhere in the description of

---

2. A single dot after a tense vowel symbol means that the vowel is 'half-long', i.e. neither as short as [o] nor as long as [oː]. Such vowels occur in word-final position, cf. Chapter 6. Most pronouncing dictionaries transcribe this vowel as short.

the language. That some morphemes, such as *aber* [ʔɑ:bɐ], only show [ɐ], and not [−əʀ], is a distributional quirk.

The diphthongs [aɪ], [aʊ], [ɔ̈y]. With minimal pairs it is easy to show that we have to do with contrastive units, e.g.

[aɪ]	heilen	[ɔ̈y]	heulen
	leiten		läuten
[aɪ]	Mais	[aʊ]	Maus
	Leine		Laune
[aʊ]	lauten	[ɔ̈y]	läuten
	schauen		scheuen

Hence, the three phonemes /aɪ/, /aʊ/ and ɔy/ can be set up for German. Table 4.4 sums up the system of vowel contrasts.

Table 4.4 The vowel phonemes of Modern Standard German.

		Front unrounded	Front rounded	Central	Back unrounded	Back rounded	Diphthongs
High	Tense	/i:/	/y:/			/u:/	
	Lax	/ɪ/	/ʏ/			/ʊ/	
Mid	Tense	/e:/	/ø:/	/ə/		/o:/	
	Lax	/ɛ/	/œ/			/ɔ/	/ɔy/
		/ɛ:/					
Low				/a/	/ɑ:/		/aɪ/ /aʊ/

4.4 For the advanced student: Areas of controversy. In the foregoing discussion, the phonological system of German has been set up based on the method of minimal pairs. Not all of the conclusions reached find agreement among linguistic analysts, however. The following paragraphs treat some major points of controversy which continue to divide scholars of German: (1) the analysis of the velar nasal [ŋ]; (2) the analysis of the diphthongs; (3) [ç] and [x]; and (4) length vs. tenseness.

4.4.1 [ŋ]. The limited distribution of [ŋ] has led a number of analysts to consider a different phonological interpretation than the one that has been proposed here. Basically, the alternate interpretation considers [ŋ] as the 'output' of a consonant cluster /ng/. When the phoneme /n/ occurs before /g/, the automatic phonetic representation is [ŋ], since [n] never occurs before [g]. What arguments are used to support this interpretation?

(1) It makes the description of the phonological system simpler. The occurrence of the velar nasal [ŋ] can be predicted simply by positing an underlying, or phonemic sequence /ng/.

(2) It accords with certain universals of language. Languages with nasals always have /m/ and /n/. No language simply has [ŋ] without one of the other two. The velar nasal is less usual in languages; hence its limited

distribution in German is not surprising. This fact can be incorporated into a description of German by allowing [ŋ] to be derived by rule from the cluster /ng/, rather than setting up a separate phoneme.

(3) Often one hears, especially in North Germany, a [k] after [ŋ] as in *lang* [laŋk] and *Übung* [ʔyːbuŋk]. This would seem to support the interpretation of phonemic /ng/, since /g/ always becomes voiceless and fortis at the end of the word (cf. Chapter 6 for a discussion of this regularity in German).

(4) The cluster /ng/ is structurally parallel to /mb/ and /nd/. None of these three clusters occurs in initial position; and only short vowels appear before them. Positing /ng/ rather than /ŋ/ would account for this regularity. In German, virtually all consonant clusters within the same morpheme are preceded by a lax vowel.

The arguments for assigning [ŋ] phonemic status can be summarized as follows.

(1) The nasal [ŋ] is found in contrast with [m] and [n] in the same environment. It is thus less complicated to assume a three-way contrast among the nasals (/m/ vs. /n/ vs. /ŋ/) than a two-way contrast plus a rule which converts /ng/ to [ŋ]. The question as to which solution is simpler fails to define what is meant by 'simplicity'.

(2) If the phonology of a language is taken to represent in some sense what speakers 'know' tacitly, then an /ng/ interpretation does not appear to have much psychological validity. Do speakers of German somehow represent velar nasal by /ng/ and then convert it to [ŋ]? The evidence offered in favor of this position cites forms such as [laŋk] and [ʔyːbuŋk], where [k] is the result of the devoicing and fortition of /g/. Such pronunciations are not considered standard, of course. If /ng/ is a possible interpretation for the dialects with final [–ŋk], it is not a possible interpretation for speakers who do not have the [–ŋk] and it is not a possible interpretation for the standard language.

(3) The structural parallelism with the other nasals is not complete. Even where *lang* is pronounced with final [k], *lange* is not [laŋgə], but [laŋə], whereas in *Bund*, the consonant cluster /nd/ remains intact regardless of the environment: *Bund* [bunt], *Bunde* [bundə]. Unanswered, furthermore, is the question as to what degree a concept such as 'structural parallelism' among the nasals should override the simple commutation test (the method of minimal pairs). One could also argue that positing only the two phonemes /m/ and /n/ would destroy the structural parallelism with the stops /p t k/ and /b d g/, where labial, alveolar and velar points of articulation are represented.

The debate on this topic is not concluded. Linguists continue to argue both points of view as new theoretical positions are adopted. We are treating [ŋ] as a phoneme here, primarily because of the positive result of the commutation test.

4.4.2 The diphthongs. The major question which has divided analysts is whether the diphthongs are to be considered as a single unit (the monophonemic solution adopted earlier) or as the combination of two vowels (the biphonemic solution).

Arguments for the monophonemic solution:

(1) The second vowel represents an approximation. What is represented phonemically as /aɪ/ may actually be realized as [ae̞] for any given 'rendering' of this diphthong.

(2) The diphthong is articulated as a single movement and constitutes only one syllable, never two, regardless of the environment. The occurrence of [ɪ], [y], and [ʊ] in /aɪ/, /ɔy/, and /aʊ/, respectively, is conditioned entirely by their linkage to the preceding vowel. Furthermore, it should be recalled that the representation of the diphthong is a graphic device indicating beginning and end points. The tongue moves through the articulatory space of several vowels.

(3) In no other context in German do tense and lax monophthongs of different heights, i.e. [e] and [ɪ], [o] and [ʊ], [ø] and [y], form allophones of one phoneme. This allophonic variation is unique to the diphthongs; hence they should not be analyzed as the combination of two monophthongs.

Arguments for the biphonemic solution.

(1) Since it is a question in every case of the 'same' diphthong phonemically, we may represent it with one symbolization and note the various realizations of it, just as for the monophthongs. The diphthong /aɪ/, for example, has as possible allophones [aɪ] and [ae̞], among others.

(2) Distributional argument: minimal pairs can be found in which the second member of the diphthong contrasts with some other phoneme in German, for example:

Main vs. Mann	/ɪ/ vs. /n/
Feile vs. Falle	/ɪ/ vs. /l/
Eule vs. Elle	/y/ vs. /l/

(Pairs such as *Haus* vs. *Hals* are not quite minimal, since the diphthong has the vowel [a], the monophthong [a].)

We have considered the arguments for the monophonemic solution more compelling, since most of our evidence for setting up phonemes is based on the phonetic evidence rather than on distributional patterns. The same reasoning was used earlier to favor the inclusion of /ŋ/ as a phoneme. The distributional argument here assumes that there is an identity between the second element of the diphthong and already established monophthongal phonemes, but phonetically we are dealing with a continuum, not with two sounds.

4.4.3 [ç] and [x]. This seems to be a classic instance of complementary distribution, were it not for some putative minimal pairs involving the suffix −chen ([−çen]: Kuhchen [kʰuːçen] 'little cow' versus Kuchen [kʰuːxən], and Tauchen 'little rope' versus tauchen. These examples would seem to dictate that [ç] and [x] be classified as two phonemes, since both sounds occur after a back vowel. Some analysts object that the two examples, Kuhchen and Tauchen, are simply made-up forms, which many speakers find distinctly odd. But dictionaries do give Frauchen 'little woman' and Grauchen 'little donkey' as acceptable words which show the occurrence of [ç] after the 'backing' diphthong, even if no minimal pairs can be found.

It is worth pausing here a moment to reflect on the method that has been used in this discussion, the method of minimal pairs. Reliable results are obtained as long as the language gives the kind of data for which the method is suited. Sometimes, as in the case of /ʃ/ and /ʒ/, the lexical material is simply not there, as it is for, say, /p/ and /b/. In that case, the decision was made to consider /ʒ/ a phoneme for other reasons. The method of minimal pairs is one very good device for discovering the contrasts in a language, but it need not be the only one. In the present case, its strict application gives a result whereby a handful of apparent exceptions, some of which are questionable words at that, cancels a very large number of regularities. Literally hundreds of examples show [ç] and [x] in complementary distribution. Two or three exceptions, all involving the suffix -chen, constitute a deviation from this pattern. Must one nonetheless hold strictly to the method of minimal pairs?

Some linguists would answer the question in the affirmative. Others see no objection to bringing in other factors, other components of the language, which have a bearing on the phonological analysis of a language. In the present case, some morphological information can be employed. It has been observed that when the phoneme /x/ occurs in morpheme-initial position, it is pronounced as the palatal [ç]. This holds not only for -chen, but also for those words where /x/ occurs in word-initial position, e.g. Charisma, Chemie, Cherub, Chiasmus, China, Chirurg, etc. Hence, if the statement regarding the distribution of [ç] and [x] is amended to include '[ç] after a morpheme boundary', then [ç] and [x] can be regarded as variants of one phoneme.

4.4.4 The problem: Length vs. tenseness. Analysts have long disagreed on which of the two features—length or tenseness—should be considered primary in setting up the phonemes of the vowel system. Is it the case that tense vowels BECOME LONG when stressed, or do long vowels BECOME SHORT when unstressed? For example, should Juwel be represented as /juːˈveːl/, which phonetically becomes [juˈveːl] when stress is assigned to the second syllable? Or is the phonemic representation /juvel/, which has the second vowel long when actually pronounced? Are the tense vowels to be represented phonemically as /i e y ø u o/ or as /iː eː yː øː uː oː/?

Arguments for considering tenseness primary:

(1) The distinction between 'tense' and 'lax' vowels is always maintained regardless of the environment, whereas length is dependent on some other factor, namely, the presence of stress. Vowels are thus inherently tense or lax, but only lax vowels are inherently short.

(2) A number of so-called 'function words', such as pronouns and prepositions, are not normally stressed, and thus should be represented phonemically with a short, tense vowel, e.g. *der* [deɐ̯], *dem* [dem], *den* [den], *ihn* [im], *sie* [zi], *über* [ybɐ̯], etc. Only when they occur in emphatic position is the vowel long.

Arguments for considering length primary:

(1) In normal rapid speech, tense unstressed vowels tend to become pronounced like short, lax vowels, e.g. *Juwel* is often pronounced [juve:l](instead of [juve:l]), and [hɔlʊndɐ̯] for [holʊndɐ̯](*Holunder*). The phonetic transcriptions of the pronouncing dictionaries tend to be idealized in this respect. This would confirm the hypothesis that length is distinctive, since shortness tends to be correlated automatically with laxness in these words. Thus, the distinction between tense and lax vowels is not always maintained in actual speech.

(2) Two phonemes, /ɛ:/ and /ɑ:/, are long, but not tense. They, too, are affected by the placement of stress. In unstressed syllables they become short. If a general rule is devised, whereby all long vowels become short when not stressed, then tense vowels, as well as /ɛ:/ and /ɑ:/, are included. Otherwise, two generalizations must be made, one for tense vowels (which become long when stressed), and one for /ɛ:/ and /ɑ:/, which become short when unstressed.

In this book, length is considered primary, that is, all tense vowels are marked long in their underlying (=phonemic) representation. All long vowels—tense vowels as well as /ɛ:/ and /ɑ:/—regularly become short when they are not under stress. This is the simplest way of stating the correlation between stress and length.

Further reading

Recent books which treat the phonology of Modern German include:

Kohler, Klaus. 1977. Einführung in die Phonetik des Deutschen. Berlin: Schmidt.

Meinhold, Gottfried, and Eberhard Stock. 1980. Phonologie der deutschen Gegenwartssprache. Leipzig: VEB Bibliographisches Institut.

Philipp, Marthe. 1974. Phonologie des Deutschen. Stuttgart: Kohlhammer.

Although all are billed as introductions, each presents different degrees of difficulty and interest. Meinhold and Stock, for example, introduce historical information; Phillip's theoretical orientation omits any discussion of prosody.

A very brief overview of German phonology is found in Chapter 10 of:

Herbst, Thomas, David Heath, and Hans-Martin Dedering, eds. 1979. Grimm's grandchildren. Current topics in German linguistics. London and New York: Longmans.

A survey of the major problems in the phonological description of German with the various suggestions for solutions is represented in:

Werner, Otmar. 1972. Phonemik des Deutschen. Stuttgart: Metzler. (Sammlung Metzler, Band 108.)

General books on phonological theory can be divided into several theoretical schools. Overviews of the current situation in phonology are represented by:

Dinnsen, Daniel A. 1979. Current approaches to phonological theory. Bloomington: Indiana University.
Sommerstein, Alan H. 1977. Modern phonology. Baltimore: University Park.

The various schools of thought in phonology are represented in the following works:

Chomsky, Noam, and Morris Halle. 1968. The sound pattern of English. New York: Harper & Row. (Something of a classic, representing transformational-generative theory; a work which virtually every subsequent study of phonology presupposes.)
Anderson, Stephen R. 1974. The organization of phonology. New York: Academic Press. (Generative-transformational)
Kenstowicz, Michael, 1979. Generative phonology. New York: Academic Press. (Generative-transformational)
Hooper, Joan B. 1976. An introduction to natural generative phonology. New York: Academic Press. (Natural generative phonology)
Linell, Per. 1979. Psychological reality in phonology: A theoretical study. Cambridge: Cambridge University Press. (Concrete phonology)
Stampe, David. 1979. A dissertation on natural phonology. Bloomington: Indiana University Linguistics Club. (Natural phonology)

A classic in the field of phonology is:

Trubetzkoy, N. S. 1969. Principles of phonology. Berkeley: University of California Press. (Translation of: Grundzüge der Phonologie, 4. Aufl. Göttingen: Vandenhoeck & Ruprecht, 1967; originally published in 1939.)

An overview in German of the basic concepts and methodology of phonology can be found in the brief (78 pages) volume in the Sammlung Metzler (Band 104):

Heike, Georg. 1972. Phonologie. Stuttgart: Metzler.

Problems

Problem 1. Fill in the phonetic detail for the following phonemic transcriptions:

(1)	/aɪnrɪxtən/	[ʔaɪn ɪ tən]	(einrichten)
(2)	frɔydə/	[f ɔydə]	(Freude)
(3)	/gəlɑ:gərt/	[gəlɑ:g t]	(gelagert)
(4)	/pʊpə/	[p ʊpə]	(Puppe)
(5)	/ɛrle:bə/	[ʔɛ le:bə]	(erlebe)
(6)	/to:rə/	[t o: ə]	(Tore)
(7)	/fo:to:/	[fo:t]	(Foto)
(8)	/mœrdər/	[mœ d]	(Mörder)
(9)	/hɔyxəlaɪ/	[hɔy əlaɪ]	(Heuchelei)
(10)	/kɛlx/	[k ɛl]	(Kelch)
(11)	/dasbɛt/	[dasbɛt]	(das Bett)
(12)	/dɛsvaldəs/	[dɛsvaldəs]	(des Waldes)

Problem 2. Find as many minimal pairs as you can for the following items. You need not limit yourself to examples from the same word class. Example: /ʃtɛlən/ (stellen)/ʃte:lən/ (stehlen); /ʃvɛlən/ (schwellen), etc.

(1) /taʃə/ (Tasche) ....
....

(2) /has/ (Haß) ....
....

(3) /ku:/ (Kuh) ....
....

(4) /hɛŋə/ (hänge) ....
....

(5) /rast/ (Rast) ....
....

(6) /ʃraŋk/ (Schrank) ....
....

(7) /gry:sə/ (grüße) ....
....

(8) /dax/ (Dach) ....
....

(9) /brɛt/ (Brett) ....
....

(10) /ʃo:n/ (schon) ....
....

A distinction that does not
further understanding is no
distinction.

—Goethe

Chapter 5
Phonology: Distinctive features

5.0 Definition. In the previous chapters, terms such as 'consonant', 'vowel', 'obstruent', 'sonorant' have presupposed that the units of the phonological system fall into natural classes, the members of which display a set of characteristics, or features, which distinguish one class of phonemes from all other phonemes in the language. In the present chapter this presupposition is formalized more precisely, assisting us to see the dynamics of the phonological system in Chapter 6. A DISTINCTIVE FEATURE can be defined as any phonetic characteristic which is used to distinguish two phonemes. Hence, 'nasality' is a distinctive feature since it separates one class of phonemes (/m n ŋ/) from all others. 'Tenseness' is also a distinctive feature, since it separates one set of vowels (e.g. /i: e: y: ø: o: u:/) from all the others, etc. One of the goals of linguistic theory has been to identify the minimum number of such features which would be adequate to describe the phonological system of any language in the world. The task, is not yet complete, however, and linguists are not in agreement as to which features should be included (see *Further reading* at the end of the chapter for references).

Original distinctive feature theory conceived of all features as BINARY, that is, a phoneme either did or did not possess a given feature, for example, voice. Obstruents, for instance, are either [+voice] or [−voice]. In more recent theory, the notion of SCALAR features has also been advocated; for example, vowel height is best measured on a scale from high to low. For German, three heights have been selected: high, mid, and low. Scalar features are more suitable for designating place of articulation, since place occurs along a continuum, whereas binary features best fit many other categories where a feature is either present or is not.

The feature system introduced in this chapter must be regarded as tentative and subject to revision as distinctive feature theory develops new insights into the way the phonological systems of languages are structured.

54

5.1 Major class features. The distinction between vowels and consonants is a very old one, going back to ancient Greece and India. Modern
linguistic study has only confirmed this basic distinction, which is present
in every language. Consonants are articulated by forming some kind of
constriction in the vocal tract, vowels are articulated with none. In most
languages, the vowels are produced with vibrating vocal cords, resulting
in periodic sound waves; consonants may or may not involve vibration of
the vocal cords.

The first major class feature, then, separates consonants from vowels.
The choice is binary: a phoneme is either one or the other. Traditionally,
only one term is used, and is then marked as either plus or minus. Here the
term 'consonant' is used. The German phonological system is divided,
then, into two major classes: consonant, abbreviated [+cons], which includes /p t k b d g f v s z ʃ ʒ j x m n ŋ l r/, and [−cons], which includes /i: ɪ e: ɛ
ɛ: y: ʏ ø: œ u: ʊ o: ɔ a ɑ: ə/.

A word such as *knappe* /knapə/ consists of five segments with the feature specifications:

/ k	n	a	p	ə	/
[+cons]	[+cons]	[−cons]	[+cons]	[−cons]	

Vowels, generally, are responsible for the formation of syllables; *knappe*
has two syllables, attributed to the presence of [a] and [ə]. Consonants, on
the other hand, are generally nonsyllabic. Hence vowels can be specified
as [+syllabic], consonants as [−syllabic] (abbreviated as [+syll] and
[−syll], respectively).

Among the consonants, a distinction has been made here between those
which offer a great deal of resistance to the pulmonary airstream (the obstruents) and those for which the resistance is minimal (the consonantal
sonorants). These two natural classes of sounds are distinguished by degree of sonority. Sounds produced with less resistance to the airstream are
more resonant and have, therefore, a more regular sound wave with a
higher perceptual threshold. Since consonantal sonorants and vowels
share this characteristic, they are classed together as [+sonorant], while
obstruents are [−sonorant](abbreviated [+son] and [−son], respectively).
The MAJOR CLASS FEATURES are thus [cons], [syll], and [son]. Using these
three features, one can construct a MATRIX, which is a device for representing features by pluses and minuses.

Features:	[cons]	[syll]	[son]
/p t k b d g f v s z ʃ ʒ j x/	+	−	−
/m n ŋ l r/	+	−	+
/i: ɪ e: ɛ ɛ: y: ʏ ø: œ u: ʊ o: ɔ a ɑ: ə/	−	+	+

The necessity of distinguishing between obstruents and consonantal sonorants is clear from the behavior of nasals and liquids in particular phonetic environments, where the sonority of these sounds allows them to function as SYLLABICS (sounds responsible for 'creating' a syllable), e.g. *liebem* [liːbm̩], *Tafel* [tʰɑːfl̩], *heißen* [haɪsn̩], where the stroke under the sonorant symbol indicates that it is a syllabic in that position. Note that it is only in particular contexts (for example, after another consonant) that consonantal sonorants take on syllabic function. Obstruents in German, on the other hand, are never syllabic.

5.2 Consonantal features

5.2.1 Manner of articulation.
Among the obstruents, stops differ from fricatives in requiring complete closure in the oral cavity. Fricatives allow a continuous flow of air. If we use the term CONTINUANT [cont] to differentiate these two classes of sounds, then stops are [−cont]. This term is also applicable to all sounds produced by allowing the airstream to pass through the center of the oral cavity. Hence, /r/ and /h/, among the consonants, would also be marked as [+cont].

Feature	[cons]	[syll]	[son]	[cont]
/p t k b d g/	+	−	−	−
/f v s z ʃ ʒ j x/	+	−	−	+
/m n ŋ l/	+	−	+	−
/r/	+	−	+	+
/h/	+	−	−	+

5.2.2 Strength of articulation.
Strength of articulation refers to the difference between FORTIS and LENIS, a binary distinction marked [+fortis] and [−fortis]. This feature is applicable only to obstruents, and cuts across the other categories established thus far.

	p	t	k	b	d	g	f	s	ʃ	x	v	z	ʒ	j
[cons]	+	+	+	+	+	+	+	+	+	+	+	+	+	+
[syll]	−	−	−	−	−	−	−	−	−	−	−	−	−	−
[son]	−	−	−	−	−	−	−	−	−	−	−	−	−	−
[cont]	−	−	−	−	−	−	+	+	+	+	+	+	+	+
[fortis]	+	+	+	−	−	−	+	+	+	+	−	−	−	−

The consonantal sonorants and vowels all have blanks in their matrix, since 'fortis' and 'lenis' cannot be applied to them.

5.2.3 Voicing.
Among the obstruents there are differences in VOICING. The fortis consonants are always voiceless in German; the lenis obstru-

ents have underlying or phonemic [+voice], which is often realized phonetically as [−voice]. All the other phonemes in the language are [+voice], except [h].

5.2.4 Nasality and laterality. Among the consonantal sonorants, /m n ŋ/ are [+nasal], /l r/ are [−nasal]; /l/ is [+lateral], /r/ is [−lateral].

5.2.5 Place of articulation. As noted earlier, this is a scalar feature. The feature [lab] includes all consonants articulated with the lips, hence /p b f v m/; [alv] includes all consonants articulated with the tongue against the alveolar ridge: /t d s z n l/. The feature [prepal] includes /ʃ ʒ/, /j/ is [pal], and /k g x ŋ/ are all [vel]. The phoneme /r/ is difficult to classify, since its realization as an apical or uvular trill differs from speaker to speaker. Here it is called [alv], since elsewhere the /r/-symbol designates the apicoalveolar trill.

5.2.6 /h/. Phonetically, /h/ does not fit well into the foregoing matrix. Phonologically, it behaves much like the obstruents, in that it is neither sonorant nor syllabic. But it has no locational feature in the oral cavity as do the other obstruents. It is simply the audible airstream. Hence a number of features are not pertinent to its specification and are thus left blank. Table 5.1 gives the feature matrix for the consonants of German.

Table 5.1 Feature matrix for the consonants of German.

	cons	syll	son	cont	fortis	voice	nasal	lateral	place
p	+	−	−	−	+	−	−		lab
b	+	−	−	−	−	+	−		lab
t	+	−	−	−	+	−	−		alv
d	+	−	−	−	−	+	−		alv
k	+	−	−	−	+	−	−		vel
g	+	−	−	−	−	+	−		vel
f	+	−	−	+	+	−	−		lab
v	+	−	−	+	−	+	−		lab
s	+	−	−	+	+	−	−		alv
z	+	−	−	+	−	+	−		alv
ʃ	+	−	−	+	+	−	−		prepal
ʒ	+	−	−	+	−	+	−		prepal
j	+	−	−	+	−	+	−		pal
x	+	−	−	+	+	−	−		vel
m	+	−	+	−		+	+		lab
n	+	−	+	−		+	+		alv
ŋ	+	−	+	−		+	+		vel
l	+	−	+	−		+	−	+	alv
r	+	−	+	+		+	−	−	alv
h	−	−	−	+		−			

5.3 Vocalic features. The major class features, as has been seen, are [−cons], [+syll], [+son]. Among the vowel features, place is scalar, the others are binary.

5.3.1 Manner. A number of attempts have been made to describe manner features in binary terms. None has been particularly illuminating. The terms used in the phonetic description of the vowels for tongue height and tongue retraction are adopted here.

Height features: [hi] 'high'; [mid] 'mid'; [lo] 'low'
Retraction features: [fr] 'front'; [cen] 'central'; [bk] 'back'

5.3.2 Tenseness. The term 'tense' has been used in this book as a cover term for several parameters which are related: (1) the extent to which the tongue body is away from the central position [ə], i.e. tense vowels tend to occur toward the periphery of the vowel space (Figure 2.5); (2) the extent of tongue root retraction (or pharynx wall retraction, or the size of the pharynx) which seems to be correlated with (1); (3) the relative height of the tongue with respect to the corresponding lax vowel, i.e./i: e: y: ø: u: o:/ are [+tense], /ɪ ɛ ʏ œ ʊ ɔ/ are [−tense]; [ɑ: a ə] are not marked for tenseness, that is, they are neither plus nor minus; [ɑ:] seems to meet the definition of 'peripheralness', but not the other characteristics of 'tense' vowels; [ə] is not marked for either 'tense' or 'lax', since it is more or less the point from which 'tense' and 'lax' positions are measured. Furthermore, [ə] has no counterpart with respect to which it is higher or lower. The same remarks apply to [a]. [ɛ:] has been considered by virtually all linguists as a long, LAX vowel; its position on the periphery, however, puts this interpretation in question.

5.3.3 Length. The six tense vowels mentioned are [+long], together with /ɛ: a:/. The remainder are [−long].

5.3.4 Roundness. Lip-rounding is plus for /y: ʏ ø: œ o: ɔ/, minus for the rest. The distinctive feature matrix for the monophthongs is displayed in Table 5.2.

5.3.5 The diphthongs. The diphthongs require further discussion. They are all long segments, but with the difference that features CHANGE during production. In general discussions of distinctive features, diphthongs are usually represented either as a combination of vowel + vowel, or vowel + semivowel, such as [w] and [j]. The following feature specification for the three phonological diphthongs in German is unorthodox, but attempts to capture the fact that features change in a single articulatory movement from a lower tongue position to a higher one.

Table 5.2 Feature matrix for the vowels of German.

	Height	Retraction	Tense	Round	Long
/iː/	[hi]	[fr]	+	−	+
/ɪ/	[hi]	[fr]	−	−	−
/eː/	[mid]	[fr]	+	−	+
/ɛ/	[mid]	[fr]	−	−	−
/ɛː/	[mid]	[fr]	− (?)	−	+
/yː/	[hi]	[fr]	+	+	+
/ʏ/	[hi]	[fr]	−	+	−
/øː/	[mid]	[fr]	+	+	+
/œ/	[mid]	[fr]	−	+	−
/uː/	[hi]	[bk]	+	+	+
/ʊ/	[hi]	[bk]	−	+	−
/oː/	[mid]	[bk]	+	+	+
/ɔ/	[mid]	[bk]	−	+	−
/ə/	[mid]	[cen]		−	−
/a/	[lo]	[cen]		−	−
/aː/	[lo]	[bk]		−	+

The specification [−lo] indicates that the end point of the diphthong may, in fact, be any nonlow vowel, consistent with the other features, although in the phonemic representation /ɪ/, /ʊ/, and /y/ are used for convenience. The beginning and end points of the diphthong are specified with features from the monophthongs. The diphthong /aɪ/ is unrounded, /ɔy/ is a rounded diphthong; /aʊ/ goes from unrounded to rounded, since all nonlow back vowels are round. The feature [+long] applies to the entire segment, since diphthongs are inherently long.

Diphthongs:	/aɪ/	/aʊ/	/ɔy/
Height	[lo] [−lo]	[lo][−lo]	[mid] [−lo]
Retraction	[cen] [fr]	[bk]	[bk] [fr]
Tense	[−tense]	[−tense]	[−tense][+tense]
Round	[−round]	[−round][+round]	[+round]
Long	[+long]	[+long]	[+long]

5.4 Summary. Distinctive features have the advantage of showing to what degree the phonemes of a language are alike and thus illustrate better than alphabetic symbols alone the systematic relationships among the phonemes of a language. Some distinctive features are best represented as scalar, points on a line, for example, place of articulation. Most are represented as binary; either the feature is present or it is not. Features inapplicable to a particular phoneme are left unmarked. The three major class features, all binary, are consonantal, syllabic, and sonorant. These, along with other distinctive features, are represented graphically by means of a feature matrix.

Further reading

Distinctive Feature Theory was initiated in the 1950s by:

Jakobson, Roman, Gunnar M. Fant, and Morris Halle. 1951. Preliminaries to speech analysis: The distinctive features and their correlates. Cambridge, Mass.: MIT Press. (3rd printing, 1963)

and

Jakobson, Roman, and Morris Halle. 1956. Fundamentals of language. The Hague: Mouton.

Both of these studies are based on acoustic phonetics. Systems of distinctive features for articulatory phonetics have been developed since the 1960s, beginning with:

Chomsky, Noam, and Morris Halle. 1968. The sound pattern of English. New York: Harper & Row.

Alternative proposals are found in:

Ladefoged, Peter. 1971. Preliminaries to linguistic phonetics. Chicago and London: University of Chicago Press.
Ladefoged, Peter. 1975. A course in phonetics. New York: Harcourt Brace Jovanovich. (2nd ed., 1982.)

The latter author suggests that not all features are binary. This point of view is also represented in one work on German phonology:

Kohler, Klaus J. 1977. Einführung in die Phonetik des Deutschen. Berlin: Schmidt.

Whereas the binary representation of all phonemes is advocated in:

Meinhold, Gottfried, and Eberhard Stock. 1980. Phonologie der deutschen Gegenwartssprache. Leipzig: VEB Bibliographisches Institut.

The most recent catalogue of binary distinctive features is discussed in:

Halle, Morris, and G. N. Clements. 1983. Problem book in phonology. Cambridge, Mass.: MIT Press.

Problems

Problem 1. Phonemes can be grouped together into natural classes; for example, /p t k/ belong to a natural class, whereas /p t k l/ do not. The set /p t k/ can be specified by the distinctive features [−son], [−cont], [−voice], whereas the set /p t k l/ has to be specified by *two* sets of distinctive features (technically called 'disjunction'): [−son], [−cont], [−voice], and [+lat]. In each of the following sets, determine which member causes the disjunction.

(1) /p b f v m n/
(2) /m n ŋ r/
(3) /f s ʃ j x/
(4) /v z ʒ j r/
(5) /p b t d k g f/
(6) /ɪ ɛ ə ʊ ɔ/
(7) /iː yː eː øː ɑː/

Problem 2. Many studies of distinctive features hold to the principle of strict binarism, that is, all features must be marked either '+' or '−' (or left unmarked). If a strict binarism were adopted for the vowel matrix in this chapter, how would the vowels be specified? (Hint: use just the features 'front', 'back', 'high', and 'low').

/iː ɪ eː ɛ ɛː yː ʏ øː œ uː ʊ oː ɔ ə a ɑː/

Problem 3. The following sets of phonemes are inadequately specified. Each is lacking one distinctive feature. Specify in each case what is missing in order to characterize the set minimally.

(1) /iː yː uː/   [+syll][+tense][   ]
(2) /uː ʊ oː ɔ/   [+syll][bk][   ]
(3) /p t k/   [−syll][−cont][   ]
(4) /m n ŋ l r/   [−syll][   ]

Problem 4. For each of the following sets of phonemes, indicate which distinctive features characterize the set minimally.

(1) /p t k b d g/..
(2) /v z ʒ j/..
(3) /l r/ ....
(4) /m n ŋ/ ....
(5) /b d g v z ʒ j/ ....

But that to come
Shall all be done by th' rule.
—*Shakespeare*
Antony and Cleopatra, II, 3

Chapter 6
Phonology: Phonological rules

6.0 Connecting 'input' to 'output'. Previous chapters were concerned with making an inventory of the phonemes of German and enumerating their distinctive features. The commutation test (minimal pairs) led to adoption of the inventory arrived at in Chapter 4. Chapter 5 examined how the phonemes are related to one another in a systematic way. This chapter looks at the relationship between the phonemic 'input' and the phonetic 'output', using distinctive features.

The commutation test of Chapter 4 essentially takes the position of the listener and asks: 'Are these two utterances (words in most cases) the same or different?' where 'same' is interpreted as 'semantically the same'. The assumption is that the listener attends only to what is phonemically relevant in the acoustic signal, i.e. what is 'distinctive', not merely 'different'. The different pronunciations of *Reis* as [ʀaɪs] and [ɣaɪs] evoke the response that they are the same, which means that [ʀ] and [ɣ] belong to the same phonological unit. They are, of course, different sounds, but in German they are not distinctive.

In examining the relationship between the phonemic representation, say /r/, and the phonetic, e.g. [ʀ] and [ɣ], to remain with the same example, we proceed from the question: when does the input /r/ give the output [ʀ] and when [ɣ](or [ʁ])? In Chapter 4 this question was broached informally and unsystematically. Here the formal device of the 'phonological rule' is used. 'Rule' in the sense used here refers to a regularity which arises out of the OBSERVATION OF PATTERNS IN THE LANGUAGE. It in no way suggests what a speaker of German OUGHT to do, or what the speaker DOES do, but is a linguistic device for relating the two levels of analysis which an examination of the facts of the language has led us to adopt: a phonetic 'level' and a phonemic 'level'.

The form of rules. Phonological rules generally have the form: /A/ → [B]/ C, which reads: 'The phoneme /A/ has the output [B] whenever it occurs in the environment C'. As will be seen, /A/ might also represent a whole class of phonemes, or more precisely, one particular feature of a whole class. 'C' might represent a phoneme, a class of sounds, or a boundary of some kind. For example, the notation /__V means 'in the environment before a vowel'; /C__ means 'in the environment following a consonant'; and /__# means 'before a word boundary', i.e. at the end of a word. In the following discussion, each notation is explained in full as each rule is discussed. The presentation is not exhaustive. Not every phonological rule of German is examined. The problems at the end of the chapter provide an opportunity for the student to work out other rules independently.

Finally, the convention is employed of referring to the 'name' of a particular rule, e.g. Fortition Rule, by listing the rule name with initial capital letters, e.g. *the Fortition Rule* vs. *most fortition rules* . . .

6.1 The Fortition Rule. The first example is one of the best known in German. The material is 'dissected' in four steps and then the results are combined at the end.

All of the examples of lenis stops /b d g/ cited thus far have shown the phoneme in either initial or medial position (cf. the minimal pairs *Pein/ Bein, Staupe/Staube*), since lenis stops do not occur finally. Note the following examples.

1		2	
Diebe	[di:bə]	Dieb	[di:p]
Diebes	[di:bəs]		
Dieben	[di:bən]		
Rade	[ʀɑ:də]	Rad	[ʀɑ:t]
Rades	[ʀɑ:dəs]		
Berges	[bɛʁgəs]	Berg	[bɛʁk]
Berge	[bɛʁgə]		
Bergen	[bɛʁgən]		

Since /p t k/ and /b d g/ have already been identified as phonemes in the language, it would seem at first glance that the items in Column 1 have a lenis phoneme, those in Column 2 a fortis phoneme in the corresponding position in the word. But this conclusion is wrong for a simple reason: one part of our definition of phoneme includes its function in separating meanings. In the foregoing examples, the difference between the fortis and the lenis stops does not function that way. In each column, the meaning of the base morphemes 'Dieb', 'Rad', and 'Berg' is the same. Rather than different phonemes, it is the opposition already established between fortis and lenis which is suspended or neutralized in word-final position in favor of fortis (hence 'fortition'). It is a regularity which can be stated in terms of a phonological rule:

The stops /b d g/ appear as [p t k], respectively, when they occur in word-final position.

Or, using the notation that has been introduced here, the same thing could be written in a kind of shorthand.

$$\begin{bmatrix} b \\ d \\ g \end{bmatrix} \rightarrow \begin{bmatrix} p \\ t \\ k \end{bmatrix} \quad /\_\_\_\#$$

The brackets encompass a class of phonemes, the slash means 'in the environment of', the horizontal line (____) represents the environment itself, and the double cross (#) a word boundary. Here the environment is the end of the word.

As noted in Chapter 1, the difference between /b d g/ and /p t k/ is the lenis-fortis distinction (aspiration and voicing may also play an important role in identifying these segments in actual speech, but this possibility is ignored for the sake of simplifying the exposition). Thus an even more precise representation of the same rule could be given by designating only that one feature which actually changes, since manner and point of articulation remain unchanged.

$$\begin{bmatrix} -son \\ -cont \end{bmatrix} \rightarrow [+fortis] \quad / \_\_\_\#$$

This reads: 'Any nonsonorant, noncontinuant consonant (i.e. any stop) is fortis when it occurs in word-final position'.

When one turns to the fricatives, one also finds an alternation between lenis and fortis.

1		2	
nervös	[nɛʁvøːs]	Nerv	[nɛʁf]
brave	[bʁaːvə]	brav	[bʁaːf]
braven	[bʁaːvən]		
Hauses	[hauzəs]	Haus	[haus]
Hause	[hauzə]		
Grases	[gʁaːzəs]	Gras	[gʁaːs]
Grase	[gʁaːzə]		

In these examples we see that in the same morpheme [f] alternates with [v], and [s] with [z]. The [v] and [z] are lenis, [f] and [s] are fortis. It is apparent that the same process is at work as in the case of stops. The change of feature applies, then, to the fricatives as well as to the stops, the class of sounds called 'obstruents'. The phonological rule can thus be revised to read:

[−fortis] → [+fortis] / ___#

In long hand: 'All phonemes with the feature "lenis" become "fortis"at the end of a word'. 'Lenis' is written here as [−fortis] to show that the change involves a switch from minus to plus on a single feature. Since only obstruents have the feature [fortis], the rule can apply only to them.

The Fortition Rule has even wider application, as the following items show.

1			2	
(ich) liege	[li:gə]		(du) liegst	[li:kst]
(ich) lade	[lɑ:də]		(du) lädst	[lɛ:tst]
(ich) raube	[ʀɑʊ̯bə]		(du) raubst	[ʀɑʊ̯pst]
			(er) raubt	[ʀɑʊ̯pt]
(ich) hieve	[hi:və]		(du) hievst	[hi:fst]
			(er) hievt	[hi:ft]
(ich) lese	[le:zə]		(ihr) lest	[le:st]

The phonemes in question—/g/, /d/, /b/, /v/, and /z/, respectively—do not appear at the end of the word, yet they are still fortis in Column 2. When one looks at the environment in which these phonemes occur, it is in every case before either [s] or [t]. This means that the rule which has been devised here has to be revised to account for these facts, that fortition also occurs before these two consonants. Yet before the rule is revised accordingly, more data need to be examined in order to see whether yet other environments have this effect on the realization of lenis obstruents. Consider the following:

1		2	
lesen	[le:zən]	lesbar	[le:sbɑ:ɐ̯]
jagen	[jɑ:gən]	(du) jagst	[jɑ:kst]
		Jagden	[jɑ:kdən]
		Jagd	[jɑ:kt]
Rebe	[ʀe:bə]	Rebstock	[ʀe:pʃtɔk]
Feinde	[faɪndə]	feindlich	[faɪntlɪç]
nervös	[nɛɐ̯vø:s]	nervlich	[nɛɐ̯flɪç]
brave	[bʀɑ:və]	Bravheit	[bʀɑ:fhaɪt]
trüben	[tʰʀy:bən]	Trübsal	[tʰʀy:pz̥ɑ:l]
Bunde	[bʊndə]	Bündnis	[bʏntnɪs]
Herzöge	[hɛɐ̯tsø:gə]	Herzogtum	[hɛɐ̯tso:ktu:m]
Felder	[fɛldɐ]	Feldmesser	[fɛltmɛsɐ]

Column 2 shows that fortition takes place before a wide variety of following sounds (e.g. [b d ʃ l h z̥ n t m]), in fact, before stops, fricatives, and consonantal sonorants. Yet a rule which stated that fortition occurs before all these sound classes would not only be quite cumbersome, but would also lead to wrong results, e.g. the /b/ in *blaß,* the /g/ in *Gnade,* or the /d/ in *dreist* would all become fortis.

When, however, one notes how these items are syllabified, then there is a perfect correlation between the syllable boundary (marked with a period) and fortition, e.g. [le:s.b̥ɑ:ɐ̯], [faɪnt.lɪç], [bʀɑ:f.haɪt]. That it is the position of the syllable boundary and not the morpheme boundary which is crucial, is shown by *Mägde* [mɛ:k.də](which is made up of the morphemes *Magd* + *e* and fronting of the vowel) and *Smaragde* [smaʀak.də](made up of the morphemes *Smaragd* + *e*), where the morpheme boundary falls between /d/ and final schwa. The rule can now be written in its final form.

$$[-\text{fortis}] \longrightarrow [+\text{fortis}] / \underline{\qquad\qquad} ([-\text{son}]_n).$$

Here the final period means 'syllable boundary' and the parentheses indicate that other obstruents may precede the syllable boundary (as in *liegst* and *raubt*). The 'n' indicates that any number of obstruents may occur at the syllable boundary (in principle zero, one, or two). The rule reads: Any lenis phoneme becomes fortis before a syllable boundary or before other phonemes with the feature 'nonsonorant' which occur before it at a syllable boundary. Or more simply: Any obstruent in German is fortis before a syllable boundary (with or without intervening obstruents).

6.2 Lenis Voicing Assimilation Rule. Fortition, as has just been seen, is a process whereby underlying lenis obstruents become fortis, which means at the same time that they automatically become voiceless. When lenis obstruents (which are [+voice]) follow voiceless obstruents, they become voiceless. The term 'assimilation' means that a phoneme 'takes on' certain features of an adjacent phoneme. Here the lenis phoneme takes on the voicelessness of the preceding fortis. It remains, however, lenis. Examples are the following.

abb̥iegen	[ˀapb̥i:gən]
Abd̥ampf	[ˀapd̥ampf]
Abg̊as	[ˀapg̊as]
schwer	[ʃv̥e:ɐ̯]
das *Wetter*	[dasv̥ɛtɐ̯]
das *Soll*	[dasz̥ɔl]
das *Joch*	[dasj̊ɔx]
das *Journal*	[dasʒ̊uɐ̯nɑ:l]

The Fortition Rule can be written as follows:

$$[-\text{fortis}] \longrightarrow [-\text{voice}]/[-\text{voice}] \underline{\qquad}$$
(Any lenis phoneme is voiceless when it follows a voiceless segment.)

Note that there is no restriction on the occurrence of this phenomenon. It takes place across word boundaries, morpheme boundaries and within the same morpheme.

6.3 The Spirantization Rule. The Fortition Rule applies to all lenis obstruents before syllable boundary with one exception: when /g/ occurs in the adjective suffix −*ig* / −ɪg/, for example, in *knusperig, fällig, durstig, lästig, ruhig,* etc. and in the final syllable of *Honig, König, Pfennig, Essig, Käfig, Leipzig, Reisig* and *Zeisig*. Here the /g/ is realized as [ç] in certain environments, [k] in others, for example:

	[g]	[k]	[ç]
Könige-königlich-			
König	[kʰøːnɪgə]	[kʰøːnɪklɪç]	[kʰøːnɪç]
Königreich		[kʰøːnɪkʀaɪç]	
ruhig			[ʀuːɪç]
beruhigt			[bəʀuːɪçt]
(am) ruhigsten			[ʀuːɪçstən]

The examples show that, as expected from the Fortition Rule, [k] turns up before the syllable boundary in *Königreich* and *ruhiglich,* but so does [ç] in *König* and *ruhig.* [ç] also appears when other obstruents intervene before the syllable boundary, e.g. *beruhigt.* More examples would show that [k] occurs before syllable boundary only when the two 'liquids' or nonnasal sonorants, /r/ and /l/, follow. The allophones of /g/ in this environment are:

[g] before vowels (*Könige, ruhige*)
[k] before nonnasal sonorants (*königlich, Königreich*)
[ç] in all other environments (*ruhig, beruhigt, beruhigst*)

But since there is some overlap with the Fortition Rule, our shorthand version of the Spirantization Rule can be written quite simply as:

$$/g/ \rightarrow [ç]/_{\begin{bmatrix} V \\ \text{-stress} \end{bmatrix}} \underline{\hspace{1cm}} ([-son]_n).$$

This reads: The phoneme /g/, when occurring after an unstressed vowel and before a syllable boundary (with intervening obstruents possible), is pronounced [ç]. In all other instances /g/ falls under the Fortition Rule.

6.4 The Aspiration Rule. In the formulation of this rule we ignore the fact that there are degrees of aspiration in German and write the rule in accordance with the information in Table 4.1. In summary: fortis stops are aspirated (a) when they occur before stressed vowels, unless preceded by another obstruent (essentially [ʃ] and [s]) and (b) when they occur before pause. This two-part rule can be written as follows:

$$\begin{bmatrix} \text{-cont} \\ \text{-vce} \end{bmatrix} \rightarrow [+asp] \left/ \underline{\hspace{1.5cm}} \right. \quad \begin{matrix} \begin{bmatrix} \text{+syll} \\ \text{+stress} \end{bmatrix} & \text{(a)} \\ \text{Pause} & \text{(b)} \end{matrix}$$

(Any stop is aspirated when it precedes a stressed vowel or before pause.)
Condition on (a): [ʃ] or [s] does not precede.

Standard linguistic notation encloses the two environments in a bracket as follows:

$$\underline{} \left\{ \begin{array}{l} \left[\begin{array}{l} +\text{syll} \\ +\text{stress} \end{array} \right] \quad \text{(a)} \\ \quad \text{Pause} \quad \text{(b)} \end{array} \right\}$$

The brackets indicate that one *or* the other environment is present.

6.5 The Realization of /x/ Rule. In Chapter 4 it was noted that palatal [ç] and velar [x] occur in complementary distribution: [x] after nonfront vowels (i.e. [uː ʊ oː ɔ ɑ: a ɑʊ̯]), [ç] elsewhere (after front vowels and consonants). The rule can be written as follows:

$$/x/ \quad \longrightarrow \quad [x] \quad \Big/ \left[\begin{array}{l} +\text{syll} \\ -\text{front} \end{array} \right] \underline{}$$
$$\longrightarrow \quad [ç] \Big/ \quad \text{elsewhere}$$

(/x/ is realized as a voiceless velar fricative after nonfront vowels, as [ç] elsewhere.)

6.6 The Realization of /r/ Rule. Also in Chapter 4, a single phoneme /r/ was posited with numerous allophones. The situation is complicated by the appearance of two different trills, an apicoalveolar [r] and a uvular [ʀ]. These two possible realizations for trill are not distinguished by their phonetic environment but are, at least in part, related to dialect and social class differences between speakers of the standard language. One indicates that either trill may be a realization of /r/ by placing them within curled brackets:

$$\left\{ \begin{array}{l} [r] \\ [ʀ] \end{array} \right\}$$

which means 'either [r] or [ʀ]' depending on the individual speaker, who uses either one or the other.

The trill occurs before vowels, e.g. in *Meere, Nahrung,* and *Rest* in slow, careful speech, and after short vowel before consonant, as in *hart, wird* and *Furt.* In both cases, as was stated earlier, the velar fricative [ɣ] is common in normal rapid speech, and the uvular fricative [ʁ] is also possible. The vocalic allophone [ɐ] is also heard after short vowel before consonant, and it is the sole realization of /r/ after long vowels, either finally or before a consonant, e.g. in *Meer* and *fährt.* The rule can be written as follows, where the tilde (˜) indicates that several possibilities occur in a given environment. Sometimes such multiple possibilities are referred to as 'free variation', but frequently the choice of one allophone or another is dependent on the particular speaker's sociological background (dialect area and social class), and in this sense the choice is not 'free'.

$$/r/ \rightarrow [\gamma] \sim \begin{Bmatrix} [r] \\ [R] \end{Bmatrix} / \underline{\quad} V(a)$$

$$\rightarrow [\mathfrak{v}] \sim [\gamma] \sim \begin{Bmatrix} [r] \\ [R] \end{Bmatrix} / \begin{bmatrix} V \\ -tense \end{bmatrix} \underline{\quad} C(b)$$

$$\rightarrow [\mathfrak{v}] \qquad \text{elsewhere}$$

The rule reads: the phoneme /r/ is realized (a) as the voiced velar fricative [ɣ] or one of the two trills before vowel; (b) as the mid-central [ɐ], the voiced velar fricative, or one of the two trills, after lax vowel before consonant; (c) [ɐ] occurs in all other environments.

6.7 The Realization of Long Vowels Rule. Tense vowels are long when under stress, short when not. When they occur in absolute final position in a word, the length falls somewhere in between, written in phonetic transcription with a single raise dot, e.g. *Solo* [zo:lo·] and *Kaffee* [kʰafe·]. The realization of the low vowel /ɑ:/, however, is subject to two conditions where the rule does not apply: (1) a grammatical condition: before a plural marker the vowel remains long, e.g. in *Klimas* [kʰli:mɑ:s], *Klimate* [kʰli:mɑ:tə]; and (2) a phonological condition: before a final sonorant there is no shortening. This latter restriction on the rule is needed to account for final long [ɑ:] in a number of nouns, such as *Baldrian, Enzian, Grobian, Pakistan, Pavian, Pelikan, Ozean, Januar, Februar* (some of which may be pronounced alternatively with stress on the final syllable), as well as the suffixes *−sam, −sal,* and *−bar.* If neither of these two conditions is present in unstressed position, then the vowel is realized as the central [a]. The rule can be written as follows.

$$/V:/ \rightarrow [V·] \underline{\qquad} \# \qquad (a)$$
$$[-stress]$$
$$\rightarrow [V] \underline{\qquad} \text{otherwise} \quad (b)$$
$$[-stress]$$

(Long vowels become half-long when they are unstressed in word-final position; they become short in other unstressed positions.)
Conditions: (a) does not apply to /ɑ:/ before plural ending or before a sonorant.
(b) /ɑ:/ is realized in this environment as [a].

The seven rules presented thus far—Fortition, Lenis Voicing Assimilation, Spirantization, Aspiration, and the Realization of /x/, /r/, and Long Vowels—all specify the allophones of phonemes or classes of phonemes. The remaining rules treat the loss of schwa and the syllabification and assimilation of sonorants in connection with schwa deletion.

6.8 Schwa Deletion Rule. Schwa (/ə/) behaves like no other vowel in the German sound system due to the possibility of its being deleted entirely in certain environments. The various conditions for deletion are quite complex. Furthermore, whether schwa is pronounced or not depends in some environments on the speech tempo and the style of speaking (roughly 'formal' versus 'informal'). Table 6.1 shows the occurrence of schwa before /m n l/ (/ŋ/ does not occur after schwa and /r/ has been treated in 6.6, but cf. what follows). The chart indicates the usual pronunciation and not the hyper-correct pronunciation of stage speech, in which the schwa is pronounced. Schwa is deleted before /m/ after fricatives, before /n/ after obstruents, and before /l/ after all consonants when the sonorants occur word-finally or are themselves followed by another consonant. Schwa before /r/ in this environment is always deleted (and /r/ is realized as [ɐ]; cf. the rule in 6.6, part (c)). The following rule sums up schwa deletion as sketched in Table 6.1.

Table 6.1 Deletion of schwa before sonorants word-finally and before sonorants before a following consonant (boxed area) (Source: Der Große Duden, *Aussprachewörterbuch*, Bd. 6, pp. 32-37; used by permission of the publisher).

Preceding segment	/ə/ + Sonorant			Examples
	/m/	/n/	/l/	
Stop	dɛɐ̯bəm	ha:bn̩ (ha:bm̩)	he:bl̩	derbem, haben, Hebel
	fa:dəm	fa:dn̩	mɪtl̩	fadem, Faden, Mittel
	kaɐ̯gəm	le:gn̩ (le:gŋ̍)	vɪkl̩n	kargem, legen, wickeln
Fricative	gʁo:sm̩	gʁo:sn̩	gaɪ̯zl̩	großem, großen, Geisel
	lo:zm̩	laxn̩dəs	kʰaxl̩n	losem, lachendes, Kacheln
Nasal	dʏnəm	nɛnən	tʰunl̩s	dünnem, nennen, Tunnels
	ʔɛŋəm	faŋən	ʔɛŋl̩	engem, fangen, Engel
Obstruent + Nasal		ʔatmən		atmen
Liquid	fɔləm	fɔlən		vollem, vollen
	dʏrəm	dʏrən		dürrem, dürren
Obstruent + Liquid	ʔandrəm	ʔandrən		anderem, anderen
Vowel	raʊ̯əm	ʃte:ən	grɔʏ̯əl	rauhem, stehen, Greuel

$$/\text{ə}/ \quad \rightarrow \quad \text{ø} \bigg/ \begin{array}{l} \left[\begin{array}{l} -\text{son} \\ +\text{cont} \end{array}\right] \quad \underline{\quad} \text{ m} \\ [-\text{son}] \quad \underline{\quad} \text{ n} \\ [+\text{cons}] \quad \underline{\quad} \text{ l} \\ \quad\quad\quad \underline{\quad} \text{ r} \end{array} \left\{ \begin{array}{l} \# \\ C \end{array} \right\}$$

When a vowel follows a sonorant preceded by a schwa, the situation is more complex. Often the schwa *must* be deleted (cf. column 2).

1		2	
/e:bənə/	(Ebene)	/e:bnən/	(ebnen)
/ni:dər/	(nieder)	/ni:drɪg/	(niedrig)
/re:gən/	(Regen)	/re:gnen/	(regnen)
/ɑ:təm/	(Atem)	/ɑ:tmən/	(atmen)
/trɔkən/	(trocken)	/trɔknən/	(trocknen)
/tsaɪxən/	(Zeichen)	/tsaɪxnər	(Zeichner)
/huŋər/	(Hunger)	/huŋrɪg/	(hungrig)

In other instances, the schwa in column 2 is retained, or usually retained:

/vandər-/	(Wander-)	/vandəruŋ/	(Wanderung)
/re:gəl/	(Regel)	/re:gəluŋ/	(Regelung)
		/re:gələ/	(regele)
/e:bən/	(eben)	/e:bənə/	(ebene)
/grø:sər/	(größer)	/grø:sərə/	(größere)

A second schwa deletion rule can be formulated for the sequence schwa+sonorant+vowel, which applies selectively, that is, it has to be specified that for some words it does apply, for others it does not.

$$/\text{ə}/ \quad \rightarrow \quad \text{ø} \bigg/ \underline{\hspace{2cm}} \left[\begin{array}{l} +\text{cons} \\ +\text{son} \end{array}\right] [+\text{syll}]$$

(Schwa is deleted when followed by a consonantal sonorant plus a vowel.)

If the deletion would result in a consonant cluster which does not otherwise occur in German, the rule is suspended. Thus, in the following words, schwa is not deleted: *Wucherer* /vʋxərər/, *hellere* /hɛlərə/, *seligere* /ze:lɪgərə/, *deutlichere* /dɔytlɪxərə/, and *Titelei* /ti:təlaɪ/. The phonetic sequences [xʀ] (*[vʋxʀɐ] is impossible), [lʀ] (*[hɛlʀə]), and [çʀ] at the beginning of syllables are unknown in German, as is a syllabic sonorant followed by a vowel; hence *[tʰi:tlaɪ̯] is not a possible rendering of that word.[1]

---

1. The asterisk in linguistic notation indicates a nonoccurring form.

A more detailed study of schwa deletion—questions of statistical frequency, speech tempo, and style of speaking—will be omitted here. The Schwa Deletion Rule can be summed up as follows:

$$/\mathrm{ə}/ \quad \rightarrow \quad \emptyset \left/ \begin{array}{l} \begin{bmatrix} -\text{son} \\ +\text{cont} \end{bmatrix} \quad \underline{\hspace{1cm}}\text{m} \\[2em] [-\text{son}\ ] \quad \underline{\hspace{1cm}}\text{n} \\[1em] [+\text{cons}\ ] \quad \underline{\hspace{1cm}}\text{l} \\[1em] \underline{\hspace{1cm}}\text{r} \end{array} \right\} \begin{Bmatrix} \# \\ \text{C} \end{Bmatrix} \qquad \text{(a)}$$

$$\underline{\hspace{1cm}} \begin{bmatrix} +\text{cons} \\ +\text{son} \end{bmatrix} \quad [\,+\text{syll}] \qquad \text{(b)}$$

((a) Schwa is deleted before a sonorant when the latter is final or followed by a consonant. The following restrictions hold: deletion occurs before /m/ when schwa is preceded by a fricative, before /n/ when preceded by an obstruent, before /l/ when preceded by a consonant, and always before /r/. (b) Schwa may also be deleted when followed by a consonantal sonorant plus vowel.)

6.9 Homorganic Assimilation Rule. Assimilation of the following nasal is the automatic result of schwa deletion. In Table 6.1, the forms *haben* [hɑ:bm̩] and *legen* [le:gŋ̍] show a final nasal which differs from the underlying (phonemic) /n/. When the schwa of the ending /ən/ is deleted, the following nasal takes on the same point of articulation as the adjacent stop. The organs which are in place for the articulation of /b/ and /g/, respectively, do not move; the only movement in the vocal tract is the lowering of the velum, resulting in a homorganic nasal (a nasal having the same point of articulation as the preceding obstruent).

The same phenomenon occurs after schwa deletion in certain past participles of strong verbs, such as *gerieben* [gəri:bm̩] and *gelegen* [gəle:gŋ̍], as well as in the adjectival forms *geriebene* [gəri:bmnə] and *gelegene* [gele:gŋnə]. The peculiarity of the latter assimilation is that the original nasal gets divided between the last two syllables.

This Homorganic Assimilation Rule is written as follows, where α, the alpha symbol, means 'having the same value as' (e.g. if the stop is labial, then the nasal is also labial, etc.):

$$[+\text{nas}] \quad \rightarrow \quad [\text{αplace}] \left/ \begin{bmatrix} +\text{cons} \\ -\text{cont} \\ \text{αplace} \end{bmatrix} \right. \underline{\hspace{1cm}}$$

(Any nasal takes on the same place of articulation as a preceding stop.)

Condition: Stop is not in word-initial position.

An automatic consequence of the loss of schwa following a consonant is the syllabification of the nasals and the lateral, e.g. /gro:səm/ → [ɡʀo:sm̩], /vɪkəl/ → [vɪkl̩], /gəri:bənə/ → [gəʀi:bm̩nə]. The rule is written as:

$$\left\{\begin{matrix}\begin{bmatrix}+\text{cons}\\+\text{son}\\+\text{nas}\end{bmatrix}\\[+\text{lat}]\end{matrix}\right\} \rightarrow \quad [+\text{syll}] \ / \ C \underline{\hspace{2cm}} \left\{\begin{matrix}\#\\C\end{matrix}\right\}$$

(Any nasal or lateral becomes syllabic after a consonant, before word boundary or before another consonant.)

6.10 Summary. Phonological rules are a formal device for relating what happens to distinctive features in particular environments. It is another way of accounting for the phonetic facts of a language, given the particular system of contrasts in that language. For review purposes, a summary of all the shorthand devices used in this chapter is detailed in the list of Symbols and Abbreviations at the end of this book.

A summary of the phonological rules discussed in this chapter follows.

(1) Fortition Rule. All obstruents become fortis when they occur before a syllable boundary (with or without intervening obstruents), e.g. /b/ → [p] in *leb, lebt, lebst;*

(2) Lenis Voicing Assimilation Rule. Lenis obstruents become voiceless when preceded by voiceless sound, e.g. /v/ → [v̥] in *schwer, das Verbot;*

(3) Spirantization Rule. /g/ → [ç] when preceded by an unstressed vowel and before a syllable boundary (with or without intervening obstruents), e.g. *willig, bewilligt, bewilligst.*

(4) Aspiration Rule. Voiceless stops are aspirated at the beginning of a stressed syllable (unless preceded by [ʃ] or [s]) and before pause, e.g. *trauen, halt!* Otherwise they are unaspirated.

(5) Realization of /x/ Rule. /x/ is realized as [x] after nonfront vowels, as [ç] otherwise, e.g. *Buch* [x], *Bücher* [ç].

(6) Realization of /r/ Rule. /r/ is realized as the voiced velar fricative [ɣ] or a trill before vowels, as [ɣ], trill, or [ɐ] after lax vowels before consonant, and as [ɐ] elsewhere.

(7) Realization of Long Vowels Rule. Long vowels become short when not under stress except in final position where they are half-long.

(8) Schwa Deletion Rule. Schwa is regularly deleted before consonantal sonorants which are in final position or before consonant. This holds in all cases for /r/; when a consonant precedes and /l/ follows; when an obstruent precedes and /n/ follows; and when a fricative precedes and /m/ follows. In many instances it is deleted before a sonorant followed by a vowel.

(9) Homorganic Assimilation Rule. Following schwa deletion, any nasal takes on the same point of articulation as the preceding obstruent. Syllabifying of the consonantal sonorant occurs after obstruent in final position or before another consonant.

Further reading

A good discussion of the various kinds of rules subsumed in this chapter under 'phonological rule' can be found in

Sommerstein, Alan H. 1977. Modern phonology. Baltimore: University Park.

Phonological Rules are discussed in all of the general works on phonology cited at the end of Chapter 4. In German, only one of the works listed treats rules for German:

Meinhold, Gottfried, and Eberhard Stock. 1980. Phonologie der deutschen Gegenwartssprache. Leipzig: VEB Bibliographisches Institut.

In addition, somewhat outdated generative accounts of phonological rules for German are found in:

Wurzel, Wolfgang Ulrich. 1970. Studien zur deutschen Lautstruktur. Berlin: Akademie Verlag. (Studia grammatica 8.)
Scholz, Hans-Joachim. 1972. Untersuchungen zur Lautstruktur deutscher Wörter. München: Fink.

Problems

1. The following phonological rules are stated in terms of distinctive features. Rewrite them, using phonemic symbols (use C for consonant, V for vowel). A non-German example:

$$\begin{bmatrix} -\text{cont} \\ -\text{fortis} \\ +\text{voice} \\ \text{vel} \end{bmatrix} \rightarrow [+\text{cont}] \Big/ [+\text{syll}] \underline{\quad} [+\text{syll}]$$

phonemic symbols: /g/ → [ɣ] /V__V

(a) $$\begin{bmatrix} -\text{cont} \\ -\text{fortis} \\ +\text{voice} \\ \text{vel} \end{bmatrix} \rightarrow \begin{bmatrix} +\text{cont} \\ +\text{fortis} \\ \text{pal} \end{bmatrix} \Big/ \begin{bmatrix} +\text{syll} \\ -\text{stress} \end{bmatrix} \underline{\quad} ([-\text{son}]).$$

(b) $$\begin{bmatrix} +\text{cont} \\ +\text{fortis} \\ \text{vel} \end{bmatrix} \rightarrow [\text{pal}] \Big/ \begin{bmatrix} +\text{syll} \\ +\text{front} \end{bmatrix} \underline{\quad}$$

Problem 2. The following phonological rules are stated using phonemic symbols. Rewrite them, using distinctive feature notation.

(a) /ə/ → ø / $\left\{ \begin{array}{c} f \\ s \\ \int \\ v \\ z \end{array} \right\}$ ___ $\left\{ \begin{array}{c} m \\ n \\ \eta \\ l \\ r \end{array} \right\}$

(b) $\left\{ \begin{array}{c} i: \\ e: \\ y: \\ ø: \\ u: \\ o: \end{array} \right\}$ → $\left\{ \begin{array}{c} i \\ e \\ Y \\ ø \\ u \\ o \end{array} \right\}$ / ___ [−stress]

(c) $\left\{ \begin{array}{c} b \\ d \\ g \end{array} \right\}$ → $\left\{ \begin{array}{c} \overset{\circ}{b} \\ \overset{\circ}{d} \\ \overset{\circ}{g} \end{array} \right\}$ / $\begin{array}{c} p \\ t \\ k \\ f \\ s \\ \int \\ x \end{array}$ ___

(d) /n/ → [m] / b ___
    /n/ → [ŋ] / g ___

Problem 3. Write the following phonemic representations in phonetic transcription. Assume that these are words spoken in isolation.

(1) /hɛftəln/   (6) /mɪlx/
(2) /haux/   (7) /plaɪtə/
(3) /ze:'nɑ:t/   (8) /'ve:gzɑ:m/
(4) /'taktɪʃ/   (9) /'kafe:/
(5) /um'vɛrbən/   (10) /buntərə/

Problem 4. Fill in the phonetic detail.

(1) Keks   [k e k s]
(2) Abbrand   [a p b a n t]
(3) Khaki   [k ɑ k i]
(4) Klausur   [k l ɑu z u]
(5) mitwirken   [m ɪ t v ɪ k]
(6) Trommel   [t   ɔ m   ]
(7) privat   [p   i ' v ɑ t]
(8) Zwietracht [ts v i t   a x t]
(9) NATO   ['n ɑ t o]
(10) BMW   ['   '   '   ]

Problem 5. Verbs whose stems end in /t/ or /d/ generally have the ending [−əst] in the second person singular present tense. However, there are some exceptions. What regularity do you find when you compare the following lists?

Ending −*est*	Ending −*st*
bindest	
bittest	
gleitest	fichtst
findest	flichtst
reitest	giltst
schneidest	lädst
schreitest	rätst
schwindest	trittst
sendest	
streitest	
windest	

What kind of rule would you propose here? Is a Schwa-Deletion Rule in order, converting an underlying /−əst/ to [−st], or does a Schwa Insertion Rule give a better accounting of the facts, where underlying /−st/ becomes [−əst]?

Problem 6. Some superlative forms of adjectives have a schwa in the superlative morpheme, some do not. From the following data, state the regularity which determines which will occur.

[−əst]	[−st]
dichtesten	edelsten
ekelhaftesten	eifrigsten
krausesten	engsten
kürzesten	frommsten
laxesten	heitersten
lieblosesten	kargsten
raschesten	liebsten
spitzesten	reichsten
süßesten	schönsten
	schroffsten
	schwächsten

Problem 7. The following data show a relatively common kind of assimilation in German. Write a rule which generalizes on the data (the diacritic '∘' indicates voicelessness).

platt	[pʰl̥at]	Flucht	[fl̥ʊxt]
Klo	[kʰl̥o:]	Schlamm	[ʃl̥am]

Problem 8. Centralization Rule. In Chapter 2 it was mentioned briefly that long vowels in unstressed position may become lax, for example, the initial unstressed vowel in *Holunder* /hoːlʊndər/ [holʊndɐ] may be pronounced [ɔ]. This is fairly common in rapid speech. One could call this process 'centralization', since the lax vowels are closer to the center of the vowel diagram than the corresponding tense vowels (cf. Figure 2.5). Write a rule for centralization using the shorthand notation introduced in this chapter.

Problem 9. Many phonologists insist that phonological rules are ordered. For example, centralization (Problem 8) would be ordered after vowel shortening (and the rule rewritten to make tense vowels lax). Hence, *Epilepsie* /eːpiːlɛpsiː/ and *epochal* /eːpɔxaːl/ would have the following 'derivation':

Input:	/eːpiːlɛpsiː/	/eːpɔxaːl/
(Stress Assignment):	eːpiːlɛp'siː	eːpɔ'xaːl
(1) Vowel Shortening:	epilɛpsiː	epɔxaːl
(2) Centralization:	ɛpɪlɛpsiː	ɛpɔxaːl
Final phonetic form:	[ʔɛpɪlɛpsiː]	[ʔɛpɔxaːl]

Can you find other instances where rules given in this chapter could be ordered in the same way?

Syllables govern the world.
—*John Selden*

Chapter 7
Phonotactics
and the syllable

7.0 Sounds in sequence. Up to this point we have considered sounds as individual units or as complexes of distinctive features. In doing so, we have abstracted individual sounds from the speech chain. However, the isolated sound rarely occurs in actual speech situations. Speech as strings of sounds (the speech chain) is characterized by: (1) patterns of sonority, i.e. some sounds are inherently more prominent than others; these patterns are investigated in this chapter under the heading 'phonotactics' and 'the syllable'; (2) patterns of intensity, i.e. some sounds are given more emphasis than others; this aspect of the speech chain is examined in the chapter on prosody (Chapter 10); (3) musicality or pitch, i.e. the rise and fall of the voice, giving every utterance a musical pattern which can be hummed, for example, independent of the constituent sounds; this aspect of speech is also treated in the chapter on prosody; (4) pauses or brief periods of silence. This aspect of speech receives no systematic treatment.

7.1 Phonotactics. Of all the possible combinations of sounds, a given language 'chooses' only a few. Some combinations are clearly language-specific. German allows [mpf], as in *Rumpf*, but Spanish does not. Other combinations are not possible due to limitations of the vocal tract; that is, there are universal constraints on the possible combinations of sounds, e.g. consecutive obstruents with a difference in voicing (for example, /p d/) in the same syllable are not possible on the phonetic level. Such a constraint has already been seen at work in the Fortition Rule. A cluster /gt/, as in /jɑːgt/ 'jagt', is not pronounceable without assimilation, giving [jɑːkt]. This example shows that a distinction must be made between 'possible phoneme combinations' and 'possible sequences of sounds'. Some phoneme clusters arise, due to combinations of morphemes, e.g. the /b/ +

/t/ in /liːbt/, which on the phonetic level are not pronounceable; there are constraints on what occurs with what. Here we examine the possible combinations of phonemes. Their realization on the phonetic level is, of course, subject to the phonological rules worked out in Chapter 6.

How large must the linguistic unit be in order to capture exhaustively all the possible combinations of phonemes? This depends somewhat on the purpose one has in mind. This investigation is limited to the syllable, which is provisionally defined as a vowel with consonants or consonant clusters possibly occurring on either side. Adopting such a definition eliminates the fortuitous combinations of phonemes which occur across word boundaries, e.g. /rh/, as in the phrase *der Hase,* or /td/ in . . . *Rat, der . . .* or /sz/ in *das Singen.* Subsequently, one can ascertain whether limiting the investigation to a syllable-sized unit has resulted in omitting any possible sequences of phonemes.

7.1.1 Sequences of vowels. Clusters of syllabic monophthongs do not by definition occur tautosyllabically (in the same syllable). Combinations such as /aɔ/ in *Chaos* and /aɪ/ in *prosaisch* always have a syllable boundary between them, or only one is syllabic, as in *Familie* [faˈmiːli̯ə]. The monosyllabic word may consist of a single phoneme, e.g. /aɪ/ 'Ei', but this is rare. Most consist of a vowel with consonants, either preceding or following or both. Here we are concerned with the general patterns rather than with every possible combination of vowel and consonant(s).

7.1.2 Consonants preceding the vowel. In German, the single consonants /x/ and /ŋ/ never occur in word-initial position preceding the vowel; /s/ only rarely occurs in that position. The phonemes /h, z, ʒ/ and /j/ never occur in clusters but only singly. The remainder of the consonantal phonemes may occur singly or in clusters. Table 7.1 gives an overview of the possible clusters.

From Table 7.1 it is clear that the number of three-member clusters is limited to six: /ʃpl/, /pfl/, /ʃpr/, /ʃtr/, /pfr/, and /tsv/. (The cluster /sts/ is virtually limited to the one morpheme /stseːn/ in *Szene, szenisch, Inszenierung.*) The clusters below the double line occur very rarely; in some instances, only a single word or name is attested with the cluster indicated.

7.1.3 Consonants following the vowel. In monosyllabic words, /h/ and /j/ do not occur following the vowel. Only rarely do they stand after the vowel in polysyllabic words, e.g. *Ahorn, Boje, Major, Majestät,* and then always in syllable-initial position. All other consonantal phonemes may occur after vowel. Cluster combinations are more numerous than those occurring before the vowel, largely due to the use of /t/ and /st/ as inflectional markers on verbs and of /s/ as a genitive ending and as a 'linking morpheme' (as in *Stiftskirche*). Table 7.2 is arranged with an obstruent as a kind of 'pivot'. A sonorant may precede, certain obstruents may follow;

Table 7.1 Tautosyllabic consonant clusters before vowel. Parentheses indicate that the cluster is rare.

ʃ	p	l	Sport Spleiß schlau Plan
p	f		Pfau Pflug Fleck
	(s)		Slave
	k		Klang
	b		blank
	g		Glanz
ʃ	p	r	Spiel Sproß Schrank Prunk
	t		still streng treu
p	f		Pfund Pfrund Prunk Freund
	ʃ		Schreck
	k		Kram
	b		Brand
	d		Drill
	g		Gram
	(v)		Wrack
	ʃ	m	schmal
	(s)		Smog
	k	n	Knie
	g		Gnade
	ʃ		Schnee
	(p)		Pneu
	(s)		Snob
t	s	v	zwei Zorn
	ʃ		schwarz
	k		Qual
	p	(ʃ)	Pschorr
		(s)	Psalm
(s)	t		Szene Tschüs
	k		Skat Xanten

a special column is devoted to /s/, /t/, and /st/. The obstruent column is illustrated primarily by the fortis consonants /p t k f s ʃ x/ since these have a wider distribution in clusters than the corresponding lenis phonemes. In many cases, of course, the corresponding lenis would also be possible, e.g. *herb, gelb; Feld, Hemd, Hand, Herd; arg, Balg; Nerv.* Table 7.2 reads from left to right: first, examples are given of the combination sonorant plus obstruent, then sonorant plus two obstruents, then sonorant plus 3-4 obstruents and finally, clusters of obstruents beginning with the fortis consonants /p t k f s ʃ x/ and /l/. Blanks indicate that no examples exist. The zero sign (∅) is used when illustrating consonant clusters without an initial sonorant. Table 7.3 shows consonant clusters with two sonorants followed by one or more obstruents.

Since this investigation has been limited to monosyllables, no examples with /ə/ occurred. Schwa, however, appears before a much more restricted set of consonants and clusters, namely, /t/ *(find)et*, /st/ *(find)est*, /m/ *(At)-em*, /rn/ *(wand)ern*, /ln/ *(wand)eln*, /lt/ *(wand)elt*, /rl/ *(wand)ert*, /rst/ *(wand)erst*, /lst/ *(wand)elst*, and /nd/ *(end)end.*

7.2 The syllable. In the discussion of phonotactics we provisionally adopted the definition of syllable as a vowel with consonants optionally occurring on either side of it. This rather crude definition obscures the great difficulty linguists have had in trying to define precisely what intuitively seems to be a very straightforward linguistic reality. Most investigators would agree that all languages have such a unit and that speakers claim to be able to count the number of syllables in an utterance (even if there may be some disagreement as, for example, whether *neuen* and *sehen* are one or two syllables long). The following statements, while not a definition of the syllable, find widespread acknowledgment.

(1) Individual sounds differ from one another in their degree of sonority, i.e. in their fullness or richness. Vowel sounds, articulated with an open vocal tract, produce a more regular sound wave than do obstruents and hence strike our ears as more prominent. Vowels are also subject to degrees of intensity, and differ in prominence (loudness) from surrounding consonants. Moreover, differences in stress and pitch occur on vowels (cf. Chapter 10).

Sonority is a relative term. Vowels are the most sonorous sounds, obstruents the least, and among the obstruents, the stops are less sonorous than fricatives. The consonantal sonorants /m n ŋ l r/ are more sonorous than the obstruents, but less than the vowels. When combined in longer sequences, what one might call 'sonority gradients' are created. In *Art,* for instance, there is a decrease in sonority from the beginning to the end of the word. In *Floh* [flo:], the gradience is reversed from low to high. In *Hebel* [he:bl], the gradience goes from low to high and then from low to high once again, [l] being more prominent than [b]. It is roughly this change in gradience which accounts for our hearing [l] as syllabic.

(2) From the foregoing, it follows that the minimum syllable is a vowel. The minimum word which can be articulated in isolation consists of a vowel or diphthong, e.g. German *Ei*, English *eye, oh!*

(3) All languages have a syllable of the type consonant plus vowel (CV); this is the optimal syllable in every language.

Table 7.2 Tautosyllabic consonant clusters following a vowel. Sequences of single sonorant plus obstruent(s) and sequences of obstruents.

Possible sonorants	First obstruent	Possible second obstruent	Possible /s/, /t/ or /st/	Sonorant +obstruent	Sonorant +2 obs.	Sonorant +3-4 obs.	2-4 obs.
r		f	s t st	(Ge)zirp	Karpf-/Knirps/zirpt	Herbst / zirpst	
l	p	Ø	s t st	Alp	Rülps/stülpt	rülpst	
m		f	s t st	Lump	Mumps Kampf	kämpft/ kämpfst	
Ø		ʃ	t st				Haupt/Kopf/Mops/Papst/hübsch/ Kopfs/köpft/köpfst/grapsch(s)t
r			s st	Art	Herz	Arzt	
l				alt	Pelz	hältst	
m	t			Amt	Amts-		
n				lohnt	ganz	(er)gänzt	
ŋ		ʃ	t	hängt	hängst		
Ø							Netz/räist/Klatsch/klatscht
r			s t st	Mark	Murks/Markt	merkst	
l	k			Kalk	melkt	melkst	
ŋ				sank	links/ sinkt	sinkst	
Ø							Keks/leckt/Axt
r			t st	Wurf	wirft	wirfst	
l	f			Wolf	hilfs-/hilft	hilfst	
n		t	s st	Hanf	sanft	...	
Ø							Stifts/oft/seufzt/trifft

Possible sonorants	First obstruent	Possible second obstruent	Possible /s/, /t/ /st/	Sonorant +obstruent	Sonorant +2 obs.	Sonorant +3-4 obs.	2-4 obs.
r	s		t st	Kurs	Durst	teilst's	
l		t	s	Hals	Schwulst	bremst's	
m				Sims	bremst		
n				Gans	Kunst		
ŋ		p		längs	Angst		
∅		k					Knösp(chen)/knospt/(ent)knospst
							brüsk
r	ʃ		t st	Hirsch	herrscht	herrschst	
l				falsch	fälscht	fälschst	
m				Ramsch	ramscht	ramschst	
n				Mensch	panscht	panschst	
∅							duscht/duschst
r	x		t st	Storch	horcht	horchst	
l				Elch	strolcht	strolchst	
n				Mönch	tüncht	tünchst	
∅							Macht/machst/ächzt

Table 7.3 Tautosyllabic consonant clusters following a vowel. Sequence of two sonorants and sequence of two sonorants plus obstruent(s).

First sonorant	Second sonorant	Possible /s/, /t/ or /st/	Two sonorants	2 Sonorants + obstruent	2 Sonorants + 2-3 obstruents
r	m	s t st	Arm	Lärms/wärmt	wärmst/wärmst's
	n		Korn	Berns/harnt	harnst
	l		Kerl	Kerls/perlt	quirlst/quirlst's
l	m	s t st	Helm	Ulms/filmt	filmst
	n	s - -	Köln	Kölns	. . .

To the initial definition of the syllable one can add little more than that sonorants may also be responsible for creating syllables. Consonants may occur before or after the syllabic, but nothing in the definition tells where one syllable ends and the next begins—an essential point, since utterances are usually polysyllabic. Which consonants are associated with which vowel in a string of sounds is dependent on a number of cues in the acoustic signal, among them duration and intensity patterns. In German, other phonetic cues as well contribute to the perception of syllable boundaries: glottal stop [ʔ] always signals the beginning of a syllable, as does heavy aspiration on fortis stops. The question of syllable boundaries is taken up again later. First, a number of terms which are widely used in discussions of the syllable need to be defined.

(1) Open and closed syllable. OPEN SYLLABLES are those ending in a vowel, e.g. *Bau, gra(-ben), fi(-nal).* CLOSED SYLLABLES are those ending in at least one consonant, e.g. *hat, Art, erst.*

(2) The PEAK of a syllable is the vowel or the consonantal sonorant responsible for forming the syllable, e.g. the /ɑː/ in *hat.*

(3) The ONSET is the string of consonants to the left of the vowel. In German, the onset may have up to three consonants, e.g. /ʃtr/ in *Stroh;* two, e.g. /gr/ in *grau;* one, e.g. /r/ in *roh;* or none, as in *Ohr.*

(4) The CODA is the string of consonants following the peak. In German, the coda may consist of up to five underlying phonemes, e.g. /m p f s t/ in *kämpfst.*

(5) The INTERLUDE is the string of consonants between peaks, in other words, the coda of one syllable and the onset of the next, e.g. /bz/ in *Trübsal,* /mpfz/ in *Stumpfsinn,* and /mp/ in *kompakt.* The interlude may also consist of a single consonant, e.g. /t/ in *Butter* and /n/ in *Männer.*

The foregoing discussion has not made clear whether the notion 'syllable' is a unit on the phonetic or the phonological level. On the one hand, listeners claim to be able to 'hear' the number of syllables; hence it would appear that the concept of syllable belongs to the discussion of phonetics. On the other hand, the determination of the syllable boundary is important in phonological processes, as we saw in Chapter 6. The Fortition Rule, for example, states that lenis obstruents /b d g v z ʒ/ before syllable boundary become fortis. The determination of the syllable boundary in the phonological 'input' is a necessary condition for the correct phonetic 'output'. Hence, the notion 'syllable' is necessary on both levels of analysis.

7.2.1 The problem of the syllable boundary. The problem of where to place the syllable boundary in polysyllabic utterances remains without satisfactory resolution. Various principles have been enunciated, three of which are summarized here and applied to examples from German. The tentative nature of these principles needs to be underscored.

Principle 1: Syllable boundaries within the interlude must not result in sequences of phonemes which do not also occur in word-initial or word-final position. A glance at Tables 7.1, 7.2, and 7.3 (section 7.1) shows which sequences of phonemes are allowable in word-initial and which in word-final position. In addition, lax vowels do not occur in open syllables in German. They are followed by at least a single tautosyllabic consonant. Only vowels marked [+tense], those unmarked for tenseness, and diphthongs occur in open syllables.

Principle 2: Syllable boundaries should be placed so as to maximize onsets (maximize the number of consonants before the vowel) and minimize codas, i.e. syllables conform as much as possible to the universal CV-syllable.

Principle 3: Specific to German: syllable boundaries coincide with word boundaries.

A few examples of the application of these principles are given here.

Graben. The segment /b/ is the interlude between the two peaks, /ɑ:/ and /ə/. Principle 2 places the syllable boundary after /ɑ:/ : /grɑ:.bən/, where the period (.) marks the syllable boundary. Placing it there does not violate Principle 1. This conclusion is supported by the fact that the phonetic output is [gʀɑ:bən] (and not *[gʀɑ:pən], if the syllable boundary were to the right of the stop).

Elektrode /e:.lɛk.tro:.də/. The first and the third boundaries are assigned on the basis of Principle 2, the second on the basis of both 1 and 2. The lax vowel /ɛ/ does not occur word-finally, hence the syllable boundary must fall somewhere after the following consonant. Principle 2 places it between /k/ and /t/ to maximize the onset of the next syllable.

Dextrin /dɛks.tri:n/. Principle 1 disallows a syllable boundary after the lax vowel /ɛ/ as well as after /k/, since the resulting onset /str/ does not occur in word-initial position in German. Principle 2 places the boundary between /s/ and /t/.

segnen /ze:.gnən/. Principle 2 places the syllable boundary after the tense vowel. The resulting /gn/ cluster is allowable in German (e.g., *Gnade, (Ver)gnügen),* so Principle 1 is not contravened.

fischte /fɪʃ.tə/. Principle 1 places the syllable boundary somewhere after /ʃ/. Principle 2 places it between /ʃ/ and /t/.

reizte /raɪts.tə/. Although diphthongs can stand in open syllable, the syllable boundary cannot be placed after the diphthong here, since the resulting /tst/ would not be a possible word-initial cluster. Furthermore, the division /t.st/ would result in an initial /st/, which is very rare in German.

Lichtung /lɪx.tʊŋ/. Principle 1 places the syllable boundary somewhere after /x/, Principle 2 specifies its position between /x/ and /t/. Note that here, as elsewhere, the syllable boundary does not necessarily coincide with the division into morphemes: /lɪxt + ʊŋ/.

7.2.2 Syllable boundaries, morpheme boundaries, and word boundaries. As the last example illustrates, syllable boundaries and morpheme boundaries do not always coincide. On the other hand, there seem to be no examples where syllable boundaries and word boundaries do not coincide on the phonological level. Compounds, such as *Rechtsnorm* /rɛxts.nɔrm/ and *Lichtschacht* /lɪxt.ʃaxt/ could not be divided in any other way according to Principles 1 and 2. In the case of *Grundriß* /grʊnd.rɪs/ and *Tierarzt* /tiːr.aːrtst/, a theoretical division /grʊn.drɪs/ and /tiː.raːrtst/ is possible, following these two principles, but in fact does not occur. In German, /grʊnd/, /rɪs/, /tiːr/, and /aːrtst/ all occur as independent lexical items. Sometimes the double cross (#) is used in linguistic description to indicate the status of an item as a 'word', e.g. /#grʊnd#/. In German, # is always interchangeable with a syllable boundary. Hence, Principle 3 can be considered hierarchically higher than the other two. Word boundaries always act as syllable boundaries, cancelling the effect of the first two principles.

As already noted, the syllable boundary does not always coincide with the morpheme boundary. When lexical morphemes ending in a consonant add suffixes beginning with a vowel, the syllable boundary falls before the consonant, e.g. *grasig* /graː.zɪg/, *Richtung* /rɪx.tʊŋ/, *Gießerei* /giː.sə.raɪ/, following Principles 1 and 2. Leeway exists, however, when obstruent and sonorant stand on opposite sides of the morpheme boundary. *Feigling*, for example, can be divided according to Principles 1 and 2 as /faɪ.glɪŋ/, *erheblich* as /ɛr.heː.blɪx/. But a syllabication as /faɪg.lɪŋ/ and /ɛr.heːb.lɪx/ is also possible.

7.2.3 Interludes consisting of a single consonant. The point at issue concerns lax vowels followed by a single consonant, as in *Butter* /bʊtər/, *Männer, Bäcker, dumme, singe*, etc. The orthography uses two letters and places the syllable boundary between them, e.g. *But-ter*. It is true that the consonants following lax vowels are phonetically somewhat longer than those following tense vowels, a fact which contributes to the listener's impression that the syllable boundary falls in the consonant itself, which serves both as coda and onset. Placing the syllable boundary there is the solution favored by most analysts. This position is supported by the fact that lax vowels do not occur in open syllables and that /-ər/ and /-ə/ in the foregoing examples never form an onset in word-initial position.

7.2.4 Morphemes ending in a vowel. Lexical morphemes ending in a vowel followed by an inflectional ending are heard either as monosyllabic or disyllabic. For example, *sehen,* phonemically /ze:ən/, may be heard as disyllabic, in [ze:ən] and [ze:n̩], but also as monosyllabic [ze:n], i.e. as homophonous with *Seen.* The same possibilities exist with *neuen, bauen, (ge)deihen, Mäher, Höher, Seher,* etc. Each may be either mono- or disyllabic.

7.2.5 Summary. The syllable is a linguistic unit on both the phonological and the phonetic level, expressing the relative cohesion between vowels and their adjoining consonants. The indispensable part of the syllable is the peak, which may be preceded by an onset and followed by a coda. The consonant sequence between peaks is called the interlude. Placing of the syllable boundary is governed in German by three principles which partially overlap: (1) no interlude may be divided so as to yield sequences which do not also occur word-initially and/or word-finally; (2) onsets are maximized; (3) word boundaries are always syllable boundaries.

Further reading

For a rather complete systematization of all the possible vowel and consonant combinations in monosyllables in German, cf.

Philipp, Marthe. 1974. Phonologie des Deutschen. Stuttgart: Kohlhammer.

Syllables and syllabification in German are discussed in:

Meinhold, Gottfried, and Eberhard Stock. 1980. Phonologie der deutschen Gegenwartssprache. Leipzig: VEB Bibliographisches Institut.

Numerous books and articles over the years have discussed the problems of defining and identifying the syllable. A brief overview of some of the approaches and definitions, as well as a new attempt to define the syllable, can be found in:

Pulgram, Ernst. 1970. Syllable, nexus, cursus. The Hague: Mouton.

Syllabification in English is discussed in:

Stampe, David. 1979. A dissertation on natural phonology. Bloomington: Indiana University Linguistics Club.

Problems

Problem 1. Complete the following statements based on the tables in this chapter.

(a) All consonants except /   /are limited tautosyllabically to the first two positions after the vowel.

(b) No more than . . . . consonants occur after the syllabic nucleus, ... when the vowel is long or is a diphthong.

(c) If an initial consonant cluster begins with /ʃ/ + stop, then the third consonant can only be . . . .

Problem 2. Syllabify the following words according to the principles discussed in this chapter.

(1)	wenden	/vɛndən/
(2)	Parlament	/parlamɛnt/
(3)	Kontrolle	/kɔntrɔlə/
(4)	Preisabfall	/praɪzapfal/
(5)	Völker	/fœlkər/
(6)	Perfektion	/pɛrfɛktsiːoːn/
(7)	planen	/plɑːnən/
(8)	Revier	/reːviːr/
(9)	speziell	/ʃpeːtsiːɛl/
(10)	jeglich	/jeːglɪx/
(11)	Rezepte	/reːtsɛptə/
(12)	Musikkapelle	/muːziːkkapɛlə/
(13)	fälschen	/fɛlʃən/
(14)	enteignete	/ɛntaɪgnətə/
(15)	Fotographie	/foːtoːgrɑːfiː/
(16)	Hannover	/hanoːfər/
(17)	Familie	/famiːliːə/
(18)	albern	/albərn/
(19)	Ozelot	/oːtseːlɔt/
(20)	Ozean	/oːtseːɑːn/

Problem 3. In one study of German phonotactics, it was found that speakers frequently simplified consonant clusters in the following ways:

/mpf/	[mpf]	or [mf]	Kampf
/mps/	[mps]	or [ms]	Mumps
/mpt/	[mpt]	or [mt]	pumpt
/nts/	[nts]	or [ns]	ganz
/ntʃ/	[ntʃ]	or [nʃ]	Mantsch
/ŋks/	[ŋks]	or [ŋs]	sinkst
/ŋkt/	[ŋkt]	or [ŋt]	sinkt

(a) State the regularity in as general terms as possible.

(b) Write a rule following the conventions discussed in Chapter 6.

-But I pray, can you read anything you see?
-Ay, if I know the letters and the language.
—*Shakespeare*
Romeo and Juliet, I,2.

Chapter 8
Phonology and orthography

8.0 The written language. Since the written language plays such an important role in modern German, it is an appropriate and legitimate task to examine the relationship between the alphabetic symbols used in written German and the phonological system as it has been described here. Orthography (Greek *ortho* 'correct' *graphe* 'writing') is a standardized set of conventions for representing a language in written form. The relationship between the orthography and the phonological system is often conceived of in layman's language in terms of its 'fit'; for example, German has a better 'fit' than English or French. Usually, this is expressed in terms of 'sounds' and 'letters', but as is no doubt already abundantly clear, the German orthographical system does not represent sounds, but at best, phonemes. Analogous to the distinction between 'phoneme' and 'phone', linguists have devised the terms GRAPHEME and GRAPH. A GRAPHEME is the smallest distinctive unit in the writing system, and is represented by placing the symbol between angled brackets, for example <a>. A GRAPH is the appearance of an actual alphabetic symbol in a text. One can say, for example, that the grapheme <b> represents the phoneme /b/, or <sch> represents /ʃ/. This is a general theoretical statement. Such graphemes are 'realized' concretely, i.e. as 'graphs'. The grapheme <b>, for example, may appear as *b* or *B* or **b** or **B**, etc. All of these possibilities are variants or graphs of the one grapheme <b>.

8.1 Phoneme to grapheme. There are two starting points from which the relationship between orthography and phonology can be investigated: (1) take the alphabetic symbols from A to Z and ask what phonemes or combinations of phonemes are represented by each letter; (2) take the inventory of phonemes and ask which alphabetic letter(s) are used to represent them. The first approach can be found, for example, in some pronouncing dictionaries (see *Further Reading*). The second approach is taken here, since the primary interest in this book is the phonological system of German. The discussion falls into two parts: (1) the representation of vowel tenseness and length; (2) the representation of the individual vowel and consonant phonemes.

8.2 Tenseness and length. A striking feature of the German orthographical system is that tenseness or length is not usually reflected on the vowel symbol itself, but rather by the use of consonant letters following. The system follows two basic principles: (a) zero or one consonant letter (in the same morpheme) indicates that the preceding vowel is tense; (b) two or more consonant letters (in the same morpheme) indicates that the vowel is lax. The two principles are subject to a number of restrictions and exceptions to be discussed here.

Principle (a) holds for all stops (/p t k b d g/) and liquids (/l/ and /r/), as well as for /f m n/. It is valid also for /v ʒ j h/, although with far less frequency because of their limited distribution or nonoccurrence in medial and final position. Examples:

Phoneme: Tense vowel (and /ɑ:/, /ɛ:/)+C: Lax vowel (and /a/) +CC...:

/p/	*hupen*	*Gruppe*
/t/	*raten*	*Ratten*
/k/	*Haken*	*Hacken, Hak-ken*
/b/	*Eben*	*Ebben*
/d/	*Adel*	*Paddel*
/g/	*legen*	*Egge*
/f/	*Hof*	*hoffen*
/v/	*Löwe*	*Struwwelpeter*
/s/	*Füße*	*müsse*
/z/	*lesen*	(none)
/ʒ/	*Prestige*	(none)
/j/	*Boje*	(none)
/h/	*Uhu*	(none)
/m/	*Dom*	*fromm*
/n/	*Ton*	*Tonne*
/l/	*Wal*	*Wall*
/r/	*her*	*Herr*

The grapheme <ß> deserves special note. Only intervocalically does it give any information about the preceding vowel. In that environment, it 'counts' as a single consonant and the preceding vowel is therefore tense, e.g. in *Muße, bloße, Stöße*, etc. Otherwise, tenseness cannot be 'read off'. In *mußte, Nuß*, and *Streß*, for example, the vowel is lax; in *fußte, Schoß*, and *süß*, it is tense.

The remainder of the consonantal phonemes—/ʃ/, /x/ and /ŋ/—are represented by more than one consonant (except /ŋ/ before /k/, as in *Enkel*), hence are unusable in carrying out Principle (a).

Vowels before /ʃ/ (<sch>) are mostly lax. The few exceptions include *wusch* (preterite of *waschen*), *Nische, Rüsche, Plüsche,* and *rösch*.

Vowels before /x/ (<ch>), may be either lax or tense, e.g. lax vowel in *Bruch* 'break', and tense vowel in *Bruch* 'swamp'. A complete list can be found in Appendix 2.

Vowels before /ŋ/, (<ng> and <n>(before /k/)) are always lax, e.g. *bringen, sang, sinken*.

Principle (b) includes the condition that the consonants following the vowel must be in the same morpheme, as, for example, in *Last, Held, Herd, Strumpf,* etc. This condition is necessary in order to account for the entirely regular instances of consonant clusters which arise from the conjunction of a lexical plus an inflectional or derivational morpheme, e.g. *lebst* /le:b + st/, *regt* /re:g + t/, *regsam* /re:g + zɑ:m/, *füglich* /fy:g + lɪx/, etc. Here Principle (a) holds consistently: the morpheme ends in a single consonant, thus signaling that the previous vowel is tense.

The exceptions to Principle (b) occur on occasion when a TENSE vowel (or /ɛ:/, /ɑ:/) stands before two consonants in the same morpheme. There are four classes of exceptions:

(i) before /st/, for example, *düster, husten, Kloster, Österreich, Ostern, Schuster, Trost, trösten, Wüste*;

(ii) before /tʃ/ e.g. *Bratsche, hätscheln,* and other words of very low frequency of occurrence have long vowel before this cluster;

(iii) before /r/ plus alveolar obstruent, e.g. *Art, Erde, Pferd,* (ihr) *wart*;

(iv) a miscellaneous group consisting of *Jagd, Magd, Papst,* and others.

A complete list of words from all four groups can be found in Appendix 1.

In the discussion of phonology, the close correlation between tenseness and length was observed. In the foregoing discussion, the terms 'tense' and 'lax' have been used, since 'long' and 'short' can both be applied to tense vowels. In many words of foreign origin, as well as in a few 'native' words, such as *lebéndig* and *Forélle,* the vowel before the consonant written singly is tense, but short when not under stress. Length, however, can be represented directly by the following three devices:

(i) by the use of <h>, especially when the vowel occurs morpheme-finally, before /ə/, and before a consonantal sonorant (however, it is not used consistently even in these environments).

(α) Morpheme-finally: *Floh, früh, Kuh, sehen* (but no <h> after *wo, so, na, je, Bö, Nu, ja*);

(ß) Before /ə/: *Lohe, Ehe, Brühe, Ruhe, Krähe, Nähe*;

(ɣ) Before consonantal sonorant: *Rahm, ihm, Föhn, Uhr, Mehl, Mühle* (but no <h> before sonorant in *(Wachs)tum, Plan, Mal* and *bar*).

The grapheme <h> is occasionally used after diphthongs as well, where its use is entirely redundant, e.g. *rauh, Geweih, Verleih, Reihe, leihen,* etc. vs. *lau, Gau, schreien, Laie, Heu,* etc.

(ii) by the use of the double graphs <aa>, <oo>, and <ee>, e.g. *Saal, Paar, Aas, Aale, Boot, Moos, Moor, Zoo, Beet, Heer, Meer, Tee, Teer,* etc.

(iii) by the use of <ie> for /i:/, e.g. *sie, hielt, mies, Knie,* etc., which is sometimes used in combination with <h>, e.g. *stiehlst, Vieh.*

The alphabetic representation of the vowels can get along with fewer symbols than the actual number of phonemes, thanks to the use of consonants for distinguishing tenseness and/or length. Table 8.1 summarizes the relationship between the vowel phonemes and their orthographical representation.

Table 8.1 Orthographic representation of the vowels.

Phoneme	Single graph	Two-vowel graphs	Plus <h>	Examples
/i:/	i	ie	ih ieh	Krise, mies, ihm, Vieh
/ɪ/	i			Mitte
/e:/	e	ee	eh	lese, Beet, Rehe
/ɛ/	e			nett
/ɛ:/	ä		äh	Säle, nähmen
/y:/	ü y		üh	Düne, Typ, Mühle
/ʏ/	ü y			dünn, Beryll
/ø:/	ö	eu	öh	böse, Friseur, stöhnen
/œ/	ö			Hölle
/u:/	u		uh	schmusen, Ruhe
/ʊ/	u			muß
/o:/	o	oo	oh	Ton, Boot, ohne
/ɔ/	o			Wonne
/a/	a			Hast
/ɑ:/	a	aa	ah	ragen, Aas, mahnen
/ə/	e			Ehe
/aɪ/		ai ei	eih	Mai, mein, Reihe
/ɔy/		eu äu oi		Eule, Mäuse, Loipe
/ɑʊ/		au	auh	Aula, rauh

8.3 The consonants. In the course of the discussion concerning vowel quality and quantity, the manner in which the consonantal phonemes are represented orthographically has been discussed unsystematically. Table 8.2 gives examples of the representation of the consonants and consonant clusters.

Table 8.2 Orthographic representation of consonants.

Phoneme	Grapheme	Examples
/p/	p pp	Paß, Lappen
/t/	t tt th	Tisch, Latte, Theater
/k/	k ck kk	Kasse, Pack, Säk-ke (division at the end of a line)
/b/	b bb	Bad, Ebbe
/d/	d dd	Dose, Paddel
/g/	g gg	Gasse, Egge
/f/	f ff ph v	Fisch, offen, Philosophie, Vater
/v/	v w	Vene, was
/s/	s ss ß	As, essen, Muße
/z/	s	Hase, Gras
/ʃ/	sch s	schon, Spargel, Stelle
/ʒ/	j g	Journal, Giro
/j/	j	ja
/x/	ch	Macht
/h/	h	Hose
/m/	m mm	Mann, Lamm
/n/	n nn	na, Tanne
/ŋ/	ng n	lang, sinken
/l/	l ll	los, hell
/r/	r rr	rot, harren

Certain consonant clusters are represented in more than one way:

/ts/	ts z tz t c	Lotse, Zeit, Sitz, Nation, Celsius
/ks/	ks chs x	Keks, Achse (where the /s/ belongs to the same morpheme as /k/), Hexe

Further reading

The relationship between German orthography and the phonetics of the language is outlined in the three pronouncing dictionaries of German:

Duden. 1974. Aussprachewörterbuch, 2. Aufl. Mannheim/Wien/Zürich: Dudenverlag. Der große Duden: Band 6, 69-104. This chapter is arranged according to alphabetic symbols. It is helpful in answering the question: Which sounds are associated with which alphabetic letters?

Wörterbuch der deutschen Aussprache. 1969. 2. Aufl. München: Hueber. 23-63, and

Siebs. Deutsche Aussprache. 1969. 19. Aufl. Berlin: Walter de Gruyter & Co. 53-114 are arranged according to phonetic symbols. They are helpful in answering the question: What means does the alphabet use to represent the sounds of German?

Problems

Problem 1. Write the following items phonemically.

(1) preisen	(14) siezen
(2) los	(15) singen
(3) heil	(16) Walfisch
(4) Storch	(17) Türangel
(5) Pelz	(18) Briefstil
(6) trüb	(19) Krüppel
(7) schwörst	(20) empört
(8) fragst	(21) befühlen
(9) lenken	(22) Biber
(10) Schock	(23) typisch
(11) Treue	(24) hämisch
(12) Bagger	(25) Ohnmacht
(13) nötig	

Problem 2. Rewrite in standard orthography.

(1) /raɪx/	(7) /fɤksə/
(2) /tsart/	(8) /riːzəln/
(3) /gərɪŋ/	(9) /hɪrʃ/
(4) /fɛrbən/	(10) /zɪŋkt/
(5) /fliːgər/	(11) /ʃpiːs/
(6) /hoːnɪg/	(12) /lɔyxtən/

Problem 3. Homonyms or homophones are words which sound the same but which have different meanings, e.g. *Meer* and *mehr*, both phonemically /meːr/. Often in German, different spellings are used to distinguish homonyms. What must be homonymous with the following words, given your knowledge of the possibilities of the orthographic system? Check your answers in a dictionary.

(1) Weise	(6) Beete
(2) Main	(7) Felle
(3) malen	(8) Sole
(4) Ahle	(9) wähne
(5) Mohr	(10) lax

Problem 4. In the following words, the grapheme <ä> is used to represent the phoneme /ɛ/: *hält, Bäcker, fällt, ärmer, Gäste*, etc. Would it be a reasonable step in a spelling reform of German to replace <ä> by <ɛ>? Why or why not? Why not replace <äu> by <eu>, since they both represent /ɔy/? Consider in your answer *läuft, Mäuse, träumen*, etc. How does the use of the graphemes <ä> and <äu> differ in the foregoing examples from their use in *ätzen, Dämmer, gräßlich, häufig, Räude*, and *täuschen*?

Problem 5. One grammar review text states that verbs with stem ending in *-s, -ss, -ß, -x, -z, -tz* add *-t* rather than *-st* in the present tense second person singular, e.g. *(du) reist (reisen), haßt (hassen), spaßt (spaßen), feixt (feixen), reizt (reizen), platzt (platzen)*. Restate this rule in phonological terms.

They have been at a great feast of languages.
—*Shakespeare*,
Love's Labor Lost, V, 1.

Chapter 9
The phonology
of loan words

9.0 Characteristics. Loan words can be defined roughly as words borrowed into German from other languages. Some, borrowed as long as two millenia ago, are no longer recognizable as such, so thoroughly have they become integrated into the 'native' stock of Germanic words. Others are clearly of recent vintage and have even retained the spelling of the original language, e.g. English *Jeans, Jazz, Floating, Shop*, etc. There is no principled way of separating loan words from 'native' words on purely structural grounds. It is a matter of historical research to determine the provenience of words. There are, however, certain characteristics which positively identify many words of non-German origin, and others which do so in the vast majority of instances:

(1) Nonsyllabic vowels which precede syllabic vowels are found only in borrowed words, e.g. *Familie* [faˈmiːli̯ə], *labial* [laˈbi̯aːl], *Studium* [ˈʃtuːdi̯ʊm], etc.

(2) Nasalized vowels occur only in words of foreign origin, e.g. *Engagement* [ʔãgaʒəmãː], *Teint* [tʰɛ̃ː], *Parfum* [paʁfœ̃ː], *Bon* [bõː], etc.

(3) The segment /ʒ/ occurs only in borrowed words, e.g. *Blamage*, *Journal*, *Giro*, *Jeans* [dʒiːns].

(4) The segment /s/ occurs initially only in borrowed words, e.g. in *Saison, Sex, Skandal, Smog, Snob;* in the case of some speakers in *Steak, Star, Spirant*, etc.

(5) The segment /h/ occurs in medial position in only a handful of 'native' words, e.g. *Uhu, Ahorn, Oheim*. Otherwise, it is found medially only in words of foreign origin, e.g. *Alkohol, Mahagoni, subtrahieren*, etc.

(6) The placement of word stress follows a different pattern: 'Native' words are generally stressed initially, except for a small group of prefixes: *be-, emp-, ent-, er-, ge-, ver-* and *zer-*, and sometimes *miß-* (cf. Chapter 10 on stress).

9.1 Stress in loan words. The last of the foregoing characteristics requires extended discussion. The assignment of word stress is particularly important since the length of tense vowels is directly correlated with it. Three generalizations, or rules, cover most instances of stress assignment. We call them (1) the Stress Last Rule; (2) the 'Latin' Rule; and (3) the Stress First Rule. As becomes clear subsequently, these generalizations require some refinement, and none occur without exception. Moreover, spelling plays a role in stress assignment, since many foreign words have come into German via the printed page, and this has helped determine where speakers have placed the stress.

9.1.1 The Stress Last Rule. Stress is placed on the last syllabic tense vowel or diphthong; or the last lax vowel followed by at least two consonants:

(a) followed by a *single* consonant (vowel is tense):

/iː/	*Kredit, Adrenalin*	/uː/	*Neptun, Professur*
/eː/	*Emblem, Hydrogen*	/oː/	*Person, Revolution*
/ɛː/	*Universität, Kapitän* as well as	/aː/	*Roman, Rektorat*
/yː/	*Oxyd, Androgyn*	/ɔy/	*Therapeut*
/øː/	*Friseur, obszön*	/au/	*Kapaun*
		/ai/	*Kuweit*

(b) in absolute final position, (in many cases a consonant is *written* in word-final position):

/iː/ *Biologie, Kommis* [kɔˈmiː]
/eː/ *Idee, Finanzier* [finanˈtsi̯eː], *Palais* [paˈleː]
/yː/ *Menü, Refus* [Reˈfyː]
/øː/ *Diarrhoe* [diaˈʀøː], *Milieu* [miˈli̯øː]
/u/ *Bijou, Shampoo*
/o/ *Niveau, Depot* [deˈpʰoː]
/ai/ *Papagei, Detail* [deˈtʰai̯]
/ɔy/ *Konvoi*
/au/ *Radau*

(c) Examples with final lax vowel plus two or more consonants:

/ɪ/	*Kommunist, Kodizill*	/ʊ/	*Kabuff, Okkult*
/ɛ/	*Korrespondent, Kolonell*	/ɔ/	*Diskont, Fagott*
/ʏ/	*Beryll, Chlorophyll*	/a/	*Musikant, Maturand*
/œ/	(no examples)		

Recall that spelling also plays a role in the assignment of stress. *Kodizill, Kolonell, Beryll, Chlorophyll, Kabuff,* and *Fagott,* for example, all end phonologically in a single consonant, but are spelled with two. Hence, stress is final.

The Stress Last Rule implies that it is the last *possible* vowel which gets the stress. Nonsyllabic vowels, syllabic sonorants [m̩ n̩ ŋ̩ l̩], schwa, and [ɐ]

are never possible candidates for stress. Note that in the following examples, the last possible vowel is not coterminus with the last vowel or even
the second to the last, when the latter are inherently unstressable:

Familie [faˈmiːlịə]   Minister [miˈniːstɐ]
Limonade [limoˈnɑːdə]   Korrespondenten [kɔrɛspɔnˈdɛntən]
deklinabel [dekliˈnɑːbl̩]   Garderobiere [gaɐ̯dəroˈbịeːrə]

Numerous suffixes and inflectional endings in German are also
unstressable. Hence the stress can never fall on them but only on the last
possible vowel before them, e.g. *Isolíerung, kommunístisch,
erstinstánzlich, Senátor, Gróbian, schikaníeren,* etc.

9.1.2 The 'Latin' Rule. The 'Latin' Rule applies to a group of
inflectional suffixes (endings) which appear on words borrowed mainly
from Latin. There are two factors which determine the placement of
stress: (1) the ending and (2) the syllabification. The endings include the
following: /-ɪs/ *(Endodermis)*, /-ʊs/ *(Stimulus)*, /-ʊm/ *(Ultimatum)*, /-ɔn/
(Elektron), /-ɛns/ *(Ingrediens)*, /-ans/ *(Stimulans)*, which are all singular.
Corresponding plural endings include /-i/ *(Stimuli)* and /-a/ *(Memoran-
da)*.
The place of the stress depends on the structure of the second-to-last
(called the penultimate) syllable. If the penultimate syllable is closed
(ends in a consonant), the stress falls on that syllable. If it is open, the
stress falls on the previous syllable (called the antepenultima).
(a) Stress falls on the penultimate vowel when the penultima is a closed
syllable: *Endodérmis, Bazíllus, Heliánthus, Rhododéndron, Dissól-
vens:*
(b) Stress falls on the third vowel from the end when the penultimate
(next-to-last) vowel is in open syllable: *Sýnthesis, Stímulus, Mínimum,
Léxikon, Desinfíziens, Stímulans, Stímuli, Léxika.*

9.1.3 The Stress First Rule. The Stress First Rule handles all the other
instances of words ending in lax vowel plus consonant which the 'Latin'
Rule does not cover, e.g.:

/ɪ/ Ínterim, Fázit   /ʊ/ Kónsul, Chérub
/ɛ/ Móped, Hérpes   /ɔ/ Éthos, Ózelot
/ʏ/ Téthys   plus   /a/ Ánanas, Kárneval
/œ/ (no examples)

9.2 Loan words and orthography. When a single consonant is written
after a vowel, the vowel is tense. This principle, discussed in Chapter 8,
holds also for the loan words, except in final position. A single consonant
there leaves the question open. In the following list, for example, the
items in the left-hand column all have a tense vowel before the final con-

sonant (which is stressed); those in the right-hand column have a lax vowel (which is unstressed).

/i:/	Katholik	/ɪ/	Fazit
/e:/	konkret	/ɛ/	Zibet
/y:/	Oxyd	/ʏ/	Tethys
/ø:/	obszön	/œ/	...
/u:/	Konsum	/ʊ/	Konsul
/o:/	kurios	/ɔ/	Mythos

When multiple consonants are written finally after a vowel, the vowel is lax, e.g. *Korrespondent, Konzert, Rebell, Beryll, Fagott,* etc. Vowels in nonfinal syllables can be identified in the same way, e.g. all the nonfinal vowels are lax in the following words: *Konkurrenz, Konkordanz, Kommentar, Molluske, Kommando, Konfetti, Porzellan,* etc.

Two other factors also play a role in determining the tenseness of the vowel.

(1) Certain combinations of graphemes represent one phoneme, and thus 'count' as a single consonant, e.g. <ph> (/f/) and <th> (/t/). Thus, the vowel before <ph> in *Philosophie* and *Syphilis,* and before <th> in *Mythe* and *Lithographie* is tense.

(2) Syllabification also determines how the previous vowel is to be interpreted. If two consonants following the vowel belong to the following syllable, then the vowel stands in open syllable and must be tense, e.g. the vowel before <kl> in *deklinabel,* before <gr> in *Filigran,* before <qu> (/kv/) in *Requiem,* before <kr> in *Sekretär,* etc. Since these clusters maximize onsets, they belong to the following syllable (cf. Principle 2, 7.2.1).

The following summary can be made.

(1) A vowel is [−tense] before <CC ... >;

(2) a vowel is [+tense] before nonfinal <C>, or if the syllable boundary precedes a nonfinal consonant cluster (/ ... V.CC ... /);

(3) tenseness cannot be determined before final <C>.

The devices of <h> as a long sign, <ie> for tense /i:/, and doubling to indicate length (<aa>, <oo>, <ee>) are highly restricted in words of foreign origin. The grapheme <ie> occurs as a final suffix in *Theologie, Chemie, Biologie,* etc., <ee> appears at the end of a small group of words, such as *Kaffee, Armee, Chaussee,* etc.

9.3 Nonsyllabic vowels. In many words of foreign origin, two monophthongs appear adjacent to one another, the first of which is nonsyllabic, e.g. *Familie* [fami:li̯ə], *Axiom* [ʔaˈksi̯o:m], *Relief* [ʀeˈli̯ɛf]. By far the most frequently occurring nonsyllabic is [i], but the other two high tense vowels, [y] and [u], also occur, as well as [o]. The boldface letter in the following words is nonsyllabic: *Partizipium, Etui* [ʔeˈtʰy̯i], *sumptuös, eventuell,* *labial, Studium, kollegial, Alluvial, Expression, genial, Filiale, Marion-ette, Toilette* [tǫa'lɛtə], *Memoire* [me'mǫɑːɐ], etc.

Adjacent monophthongs may also both be syllabic, i.e. each forms the peak of a syllable, e.g. *Kontinuum, initiieren, Diagramm, Proenzyme, Triumvirat, Poet, Diät, Chaos, Dorothea, Museum, Matthäus, Spontaneität.* etc.

On the basis of the examples from the two groups, the following generalizations can be made.

(1) Only [i y u o] function as nonsyllabic vowels.

(2) These vowels are nonsyllabic when another monophthong follows.

(3) When two high vowels occur adjacent to one another, they are syllabic if they are both either back or front. Thus, in *Kontinuum* [kɔn'tʰiːnuʊm], for example, the [u] is syllabic. In *initiieren* [ʔinitsi'ʔiːʀən], the two high front vowels are, of course, both syllabic, since they are separated by a glottal stop.

(4) With few exceptions, nonsyllabic vowels do not occur in initial syllables. This restriction applies not only to prefixes, such as *Bi-(Biathlon), Bio-(Biologie), Dia-(Diagramm), Pro-(Proenzyme), Tri-(Triumvirat),* etc., but to lexical morphemes as well, e.g. *Poet, Diät, siamesisch, fluorieren, Ruine, Pietät, Quietist,* etc.

Further reading

Wörterbuch der deutschen Aussprache, listed at the end of the previous chapter, has one section on foreign words (pp. 69-88). Duden and Siebs include information on the foreign vocabulary scattered throughout the discussion of sounds. There are also a number of dictionaries of foreign words, including:

Duden. 1966. Fremdwörterbuch. 2. Aufl. Mannheim: Duden Verlag. (Der große Duden, Band 5.)

Klien, Horst, et al., eds. 1964. Fremdwörterbuch. Leipzig: VEB Bibliographisches Institut.

Schulz, Hans. 1913. Deutsches Fremdwörterbuch. 3 vols. Berlin, New York: Walter de Gruyter. (A-Q).

Textor, A. M. 1969. Auf deutsch. Das Fremdwörterlexikon. Hamburg: Rowohlt.

Problems

Problem 1. Transcribe the following items phonetically, first determining the place of the stress. Final <VC> combinations are given phonemically in parenthesis.

(1) Akzent

(2) Melodie

(3) Armee

(4) Auditorium (/-ʊm/)

(5) Analysis (/-ɪs/)

(6) Nukleus (/-ʊs/)

(7) Bariton (/-ɔn/)
(8) Konzert
(9) Instinkt
(10) intime
(11) praktikabel
(12) Personalien (/-ən/)
(13) posaunen (/-ən/)

(14) Musik (/-iːk/)
(15) Offizier (/-iːr/)
(16) Disziplin (/-iːn/)
(17) Atlas (/-as/)
(18) Albatros (/-ɔs/)
(19) Defizit (/-ɪt/)
(20) Requiem (/-ɛm/)

Problem 2. In the following two columns are words ending in the suffix <-um> /-ʊm/, which requires the 'Latin' Rule. The penultimate syllable is open; therefore the stress should be on the antepenultimate. Yet, the items in Column 2 are all stressed on the penultimate. What regularity can you find, however, which would give a linguistic reason for the exception?

1	2
Basílikum	Apogä́um
Kompósitum	Dekórum
Máximum	Errátum
Miótikum	Karbolinéum
Opúsculum	Karbonéum
Privatíssimum	Lyzéum
Pyrétikum	Muséum
Säkulum	Palátum
Spékulum	Ultimátum

Problem 3. Generalization (2) under 'nonsyllabic vowels' states that [i y u o] are nonsyllabic when another monophthong follows. In the following examples, however, the items in Column 2 show both monophthongs as syllabic, whereas those in Column 1 follow the generalization stated. Find a phonological condition which describes the different behavior of the *i*-vowel in the two columns.

1	2
[i] nonsyllabic:	[i] syllabic:
Partizipium	Expropriateur
labial	Atrium
Studium	Istrien
kollegial	Alexandrien
Alluvial	Baldrian
Gymnasial	Kambrium
Bestie	Kadmium
Indien	Bosnien
Celsius	Osmium
Epikarpium	Insignien
Kalifornien	

Accent is the soul of language;
it gives it feeling and truth.
—*Rousseau*

Chapter 10
Prosody: Stress,
Accent, and Intonation

10.0 Introduction. Up to this point discussion has centered on individual sounds and words spoken in isolation. In this and the following chapter, strings of sounds as they actually occur in speech situations are examined. In the present chapter the focus is on stress, accent, and intonation, commonly subsumed under the heading PROSODY (or SUPRASEGMENTALS); in Chapter 11 the effects of speech tempo on the phonetic 'output' are investigated.

When listening to spoken German, we perceive certain parts of the speech signal to be more prominent than others. At least three factors interact to bring about this impression:

(1) accent, when certain syllables in the chain of sounds are heard as louder than adjacent ones (the difference between stress and accent is discussed further on);

(2) the rise and fall of the 'voice', the 'speech melody', referred to hereafter as 'intonation' (each language has its own characteristic intonation patterns); and

(3) duration; longer syllables are perceived as more prominent. In this chapter, duration is not treated as a separate topic, since it is correlated directly with intonation and accent.

These three features of the spoken language are usually spread out over a number of individual phonemes. They are not isolatable as properties of phonemes, but of meaningful utterances, whether single words or, more usually, longer strings of words. Before longer utterances are treated, however, it is first necessary to consider the question of stress in individual words.

10.1 Stress. Stress refers to the relative strength of one syllable as compared with its immediate neighbor. Although the writing system (or OR-

THOGRAPHY) of Modern Standard German does not employ any written symbol to differentiate between syllables which bear primary stress vs. those which bear secondary stress vs. unstressed syllables, dictionaries do mark the initial syllable in *Lage* and *antwortete,* for example, as the stressed syllable. For in comparison with the syllables which follow, it is accorded more 'weight' by the speaker, which is accomplished by greater intensity (loudness),[1] longer duration, and change of pitch. All three factors play a role in the listener's ability to pick out the stressed syllable in a word. An initial classification is concerned only with PRIMARY stress, the most prominent syllable, the one marked as such in the ordinary dictionary. (In this volume, such primary stress is marked by the normal phonetic symbol for stress ('), secondary stress (see 10.1.4) is marked by the grave accent (`), and unstressed syllables are left unmarked.

10.1.1 Nonaffixed words. All disyllabic words in German with /ə/ in one of the syllables are stressed on the other vowel, e.g. *träge, róter, Bálken, beréit, Geléit,* etc. Other nonaffixed polysyllabic words (words of more than one syllable with neither a prefix nor a suffix) are generally stressed initially also, when they are of Germanic origin. Since it is not immediately evident which words are of Germanic origin, the appeal to historical origin is not particularly helpful. However, the number of such polysyllabic words is rather small and can be listed. All the rest follow rules for stressing words of foreign origin discussed in Chapter 9, e.g. *lebéndig, Forélle, Wachólder, egál, Hornísse,* etc.

10.1.2 Suffixed words. Suffixes in German are divided into two groups: stressed and unstressed. Following are examples with unstressed suffixes: *lesbar, hölzern, Bäcker, zügig, tragisch, zaghaft, Häuschen, Tischlein, blindlings, Einheit, Tapferkeit, dämlich, Findling, Zeugnis, Trübsal, sparsam, Erbschaft, Wachstum,* and *Heilung.* These suffixes can also occur in multiples, e.g. *Bäckerin, lesbarkeit, Zaghaftigkeit, einheitlich, Einheitlichkeit.*

The following list includes examples of stressed suffixes of fairly high occurrence: *respektábel, nationál, Musikánt, Toleránz, Kommentár, Funktionär, Doktorát, Subsisténz, Exportéur, Fahreréi, kompressíbel, industriéll, Delegatión, negíer(en), melodiös, Planetóid, Soziálist, Sexualitát, expressív, Professúr,* etc.

10.1.3 Prefixed words. In traditional grammars, prefixes are classified as stressed, unstressed, or both. Whether the unstressed prefixes alone deserve the name 'prefix', as some have argued, is a problem ignored here,

---

1. We are investigating prosodic features on the basis of auditory impression rather than on the basis of the mechanisms for producing them. From the articulatory point of view, stress or loudness results from a greater volume of air passing through the glottis, which increases the length of the vocal bands.

and the traditional label of prefix is retained for a small class of morphemes which regularly precede noun, verb, and adjective roots. The unstressed prefixes include *be-* /bə-/, *emp-* /ɛmp-/, *ent-* /ɛnt-/, *er-* /ɛr-/, *ge-* /gə-/, *ver-* /fɛr-/, *zer-* /tsɛr-/, e.g. be*suchen*, **Be***ginn*, be*reit*; emp*fehlen*, **Emp***fang*, emp*findlich*; ent*lassen*, **Ent***gelt*; er*geben*, **Er***messen*; ge*hören*, **Ge***birge*; ver*zeihen*, **Ver***leih*, ver*mutlich*; zer*stören*, **Zer***würfnis*. Only in contrastive contexts do these prefixes ever receive stress, e.g. *Man sagte* bé*laden, nicht* ént*laden*.

The following prefixes are variable, that is, they may or may not receive primary word stress: *un-*, *miß-*, *durch-*, *hinter-*, *über-*, *um-*, *unter-*, and *wider-*.

The prefix *un-*. The prefix *un-* occurs in most environments stressed, e.g. únscharf, úneinig (adjective), Úntreue (noun), beúnruhigen (verb), úngefähr (adverb). There are two situations, however, where *un-* requires special comment.

Some adjectives (or adverbs) show a different pattern, one which is related to a difference in meaning. Where the stress falls on *un-*, the prefix is synonymous with 'nicht'. Where it does not, the *un-* is unanalyzable, that is, only the adjective as a whole has a synonym:

Deine Bitte ist ganz und gar únmöglich (=nicht möglich).
Ich finde ihn unmöglich (=unangenehm, nicht zu vertragen).
Sein Bericht klang únglaublich (=nicht glaublich).
Das ist eine ungláubliche Summe (=zahlenmäßig groß).
Die Gefangenen wurden únmenschlich behandelt (=nicht menschlich)
Das Unternehmen verschlang unménschliche Summen (=sehr groß).

The second instance concerns adjectives which have both a prefix following *un-* and the suffix *-bar* or *-lich*. Here the *un-* may or may not be stressed, whereas the root (lying between the prefix and the suffix) is always stressed:

Die ganze Sache war unabwéndbar.
Das war ein únabwéndbares Ereignis.
Begreifst du nicht, daß die Folgen unabséhbar sind?
Die Wüste lag vor ihnen in únabséhbarer Weite.
Die Verwirrung war unbeschréiblich.
Unsere Gegend ist únbeschréiblich schön.

A limited number of adjectives, which never occur without *un-*, behave in the same fashion.

Das war ein únvergéßliches Konzert.
Das Konzert war unvergéßlich.

The prefix *miß-*. The stress pattern with *miß-* is correlated with word class. It is stressed when an adjective or a noun, e.g. *míßfällig, míßgelaunt, mißmutig, mißverständlich; Mißbrauch, Mißerfolg, Mißverhältnis, Mißwirtschaft.* In verbs, it is unstressed unless another prefix intervenes, e.g. *mißachten, mißglücken, mißráten, mißbráuchen,* but *mißbehagen, mißgestaltet, mißverstehen.*

The prefixes *durch-, hinter-, über-, um-, unter-, wider-.* A glance at the dictionary shows how often the same combination of prefix plus verb may have two different stress patterns, e.g. *dúrchbohren* vs. *durchbóhren, hinterbringen* vs. *hinterbríngen, übersehen* vs. *überséhen, úmkleiden* vs. *umkléiden, únterschlagen* vs. *unterschlágen,* etc. The differences are largely of a semantic nature and are not discussed here. Only in a couple of instances is there a regularity based solely on phonological characteristics.

Nouns and adjectives with these prefixes likewise show variable stress patterns, but the following regularities can be observed.

(i) If nouns and adjectives do not have a SUFFIX, then they are stressed initially, e.g. *Dúrchlaß, Dúrchschlag, Überschlag, Úmlauf, Úmsturz, Únterlauf, Únterhalt, Wíderspruch,* etc.

(ii) Otherwise, these six prefixes follow the stress pattern of the verb they are associated with, e.g. *Dúrchschaltung (dúrchschalten), Durchblútung (durchblúten), Hinterlássenschaft (hinterlássen), Übertrágung, übertrágbar (übertrágen), Widerlégung (widerlégen),* etc.

All other prefixes in German receive primary stress regardless of word class, e.g. *ábseits, Ánlauf, aúfmachen, aússchalten, Béirat, dárstellen, eínwärts, Érzengel, féhlschlagen, fórtgehen, fúrbitten, Gégenargument, Mítspieler, náchschicken, nébenbetont, óbliegen, úrsächlich, vórtäuschen, Zútat, zwíschenmenschlich,* etc.

Multiple prefixes. When stressable and unstressable prefixes occur adjacent to one another, the stress falls, of course, on the former, e.g. *úmbenennen, bevórmunden, beaúftragen, befúrworten, dúrchgestalten, úmgestalten,* etc. When two stressable prefixes occur, the second receives the stress, e.g. *überánstrengen, überéinstimmen, voránkommen, voraúseilen, zuvórkommen,* etc.

From the foregoing section it is clear that the assignment of stress is subject to a number of regularities, albeit complex. The phonological structure of the word, the word class, the morphological structure and meaning are variously important in assigning stress. Table 10.1 summarizes briefly the assignment of word stress in German. The 'x' indicates that the criterion is relevant.

Simple, unaffixed lexemes (a) are stressed according to their phonological structure. This applies to 'native' words, such as *Blúme* and *trágen,* as well as loan words, such as *Dozént* and *Tresór.* (b) Each suffix falls into either a stressed or an unstressed category, e.g. *lésbar* vs. *Bäckeréi;* hence stress is dependent on the particular class the suffix belongs to. The same is true of most prefixes (c). The special cases of prefixation (d-h) require

Table 10.1 Factors in assigning word stress. 'Word class' refers to the categories 'noun', 'verb', 'adjective', etc.; 'Affix class' refers to the stressability of a prefix or suffix; 'Morphological structure' refers to the kind of morpheme (lexical or derivational) and the manner in which morphemes are strung together.

		Phono-logical	Word class	Affix class	Morphol. structure	Semantics
a	Simple, unaffixed roots	x				
b	Root + suffix			x		
c	Prefix + root			x		
	Special cases of prefixation					
d	*un+prefix+Root+bar/lich*		x	x	x	
e	*un+Root+lich*		x		x	x
f	*miß-*		x		x	
g	*durch-,hinter-,über-,unter-, um-,wider-*		x		x	x
h	Multiple prefixes			x	x	

more than one criterion in order to assign stress. In the first instance (d), it is a question only of adjectives which have the suffixes *-bar* and *-lich,* and the further constraint that another prefix occurs after *un-.* A second subgroup (e) requires the same first three criteria plus semantics (meaning). Words with *miß-* (f) are assigned stress according to their word class, but the morphological structure of verbs with *miß-* also plays a role (whether a second prefix is present or not). The assignment of stress to the 'two-way' prefixes (g) is largely determined by meaning, but word class and morphological structure are also criterial in assigning stress to nouns without suffixes. Stress on multiple prefixes (h) depends on the affix class (stressable vs. nonstressable) or on the morphological structure (two stressable prefixes show stress on the second).

10.1.4 Stress in compounds. Compounds can be defined roughly as the joining of two or more words (here called CONSTITUENTS) to create a new linguistic construct, e.g. *Telefonbuch, Feuerversicherung, notlanden, blutarm,* etc. The pattern of stress in such compounds is dependent on a number of factors which may intersect or act independently of one another, such as the manner in which the constituents are related to one another, the word class of the constituents (nouns, verbs, adjectives, etc.), rhythmic structure as well as semantics.

The two compounds *Telefónbuch* and *Marxímus-Leninísmus* illustrate two ways in which words can be combined into larger complexes. In the first, *Telefon-* is related to *-buch* attributively, that is, it more narrowly defines or specifies *-buch*. This type of compound is sometimes called SUB-ORDINATE, since one member is the HEAD, e.g. *-buch*, the other is the ATTRI-BUTE subordinate to it, e.g. *Telefon-*. In *Marxismus-Leninismus*, the two constituents are related to one another in a coordinate fashion. Both have, as it were, the same status; they could conceivably be joined by 'und', and hence this type of compound is often referred to as COORDINATE.

Coordinate compounds exhibit a very simple stress pattern: each constituent word is stressed, e.g. *Komponíst-Dirigént, schwárz-rót-góld, géistig-kulturéll, ásthétisch-künstlerisch, záhflüssig-klébrig,* etc.

The majority of compounds in German are of the subordinate type. The dictionary entry for two-member compounds shows the stress on the initial constituent, e.g.

	Noun:	Adjective:	Verb:
Two-Constituent	Studénten-	lángrund	nótlanden
compounds:	ausweis		
	Réhbraten	schwárzblau	skílaufen
	Schóngeist	schóngeistig	schónfärben

When nouns occur before pause, however, such as at the end of a sentence both constituents receive primary stress, e.g.

Die Astronauten quälen sich auf Rütteltischen.
Am 17. Juni 1953 kam es in der DDR zu einer Stréikbewégung.

In compounds with three constituents, such as *Lebensmittelgeschäft*, the stress falls on the initial constituent; *-mittel-* and *-geschäft* are heard as less prominent. Again, however, when the compound occurs before pause, the last constituent also receives stress, e.g.

Man eröffnet an der Ecke ein neues Lébensmittelgeschäft.

Hence, two primary stresses in the same compound are possible, one on the first constituent, following which the pitch drops, and one on the last, where the pitch makes its final drop to indicate the end of the utterance. If, however, the speech tempo slows down, the final constituent is heard as somewhat more prominent than the second, but without falling pitch; it bears a SECONDARY ACCENT, e.g. *-schäft,* in:

Ein neues Lébensmittelgeschäft ist dringend nötig,

where the grave accent mark (`) represents secondary stress.

If, now, the letters A, B, C, D, etc. are used to represent the various constituents, then the two-constituent compounds have the pattern ÁB, and before pause, ÀB́. Three-constituent compounds show ÁBC, and before pause ÀBĆ. Pause occurs at the end of a sentence, but it is also common following the compound when the latter is introduced into the context for the first time. The pattern is the same for the three-member compound whether the attribute consists of two members ((AB) (C)), for example, *Denksportaufgabe* (where *Denksport* is the attribute), or of one member, ((A) (BC)), for example, *Sportflugzeug,* where the parentheses enclose first the attribute and then the head.

A special group of three-member compounds. In a small group of compounds, the stress falls on the second constituent rather than on the first.

Dreizímmerwohnung	Dreigróschenoper
Siebenmónatskind	Zehnfíngersystem
Altwéibersommer	Rotkréuzschwester
Liebfráuenmilch	Loseblättausgabe
Rundtíschgespräch	Zweidríttelmehrheit
Mehrpartéiensystem	Althérrenmannschaft

Three characteristics separate these compounds from those discussed previously:

(1) The first constituent is an adjective or a quantifier (a numeral or an indefinite quantifier such as *mehr*).

(2) They show the typical stress pattern for attributive plus noun in sentences, e.g. *drei Zímmer (Wir brauchen drei Zímmer), rotes Kréuz, ein Mánn,* etc.

(3) None of these phrase-like constructions occurs as a compound by itself, i.e., there are no compounds **Dreizímmer, *Siebenmónat, *Rundtísch, *Mehrpartéien,* etc.

When these compounds occur before pause, the same principle holds as for the three-member compounds discussed earlier: the last constituent also gets primary stress, e.g.

Was war heute die Tageshöchsttemperatúr?

Compounds with four members admit of three different arrangements: ((ABC)D), for example, *Volkshochschulkurs;* (A(BCD)), for example, *Diesel-Notstromaggregat;* and ((AB)(CD)), for example, *Atomwaffensperrvertrag.* The stress patterns are dependent on (a) the respective configuration, and (b) the position of the compound in the sentence.

(1) ((ÁBC)(D)) *Vólkschochschulkurs, Wásserstoff-Kügelchen-Experiment, Wáffenstillstandsabkommen*
(2) ((À)(B́CD)) *Dìesel-Nótstromaggregate, MAÌN-Wíndenergie-konvertor, Kartòffelvóllerntemaschine*
(3) The third configuration shows two possibilities:

((ÁB)(C̃D)) as well as ((ÀB)(ĆD)), for example, *Ségel-flugwèltmeister* vs. *Vertràuensleutevóllversammlung.* The reason for primary stress assignment on A in the one instance and C in the other is still not clear.

In all three types of four-member compounds, the D-constituent receives primary stress before pause. If instead of pause, the speech tempo simply slows down, the last constituent gets a secondary stress. For example, in the following sentences, secondary stress occurs when the tempo is slowed on the compound.

Das ist der Sègelflugwèltmèister Hans Glück.
Sie besuchen den Vólkshochschuldirèktor in seinem Büro.

A summary of our findings for compound stress in German shows the following configuration and stress patterns.

Number of constituents	1 Dictionary entry	2 Before pause	3 Slowed tempo	Example
2	((Á)(B))	((Á)(B̀))	((Á)(B̀))	Dampfschiff
3	((Á)(BC))	((Á)(BC̀))	((Á)(BC̀))	Volkshochschule
	((ÁB)(C))	((ÁB)(C̀))	((ÁB)(C̀))	Lebensmittelgeschäft
	((AB̀)(C))	((AB̀)(C̀))	((AB̀)(C̀))	Dreizímmerwohnung
4	((ÁBC)(D))	((ÁBC)(D̀))	((ÁBC)(D̀))	Wasserstoffkügelchen-experiment
	((À)(B̀CD))	((À)(B̀CD̀))	((À)(B̀CD̀))	Diesel-Notstrom-aggregat
	((ÁB)(C̃D))	((ÁB)(C̃D̀))	((ÁB)(C̃D̀))	Segelflugweltmeister
	((ÀB)(ĆD))	((ÀB)(ĆD̀))	((ÀB)(ĆD̀))	Vertrauensleutevoll-versammlung

The patterns in column 1 can be summarized by the following generalizations:

(1) Two and three-member compounds: the first constituent of the attribute is stressed if it is the only constituent (*Dámpfschiff, Vólkshochschule*) or is itself part of a compound (*Lébensmittelgeschäft*); otherwise the second constituent has the primary stress (*Dreizímmerwohnung*);

(2) Four-member compounds: the attribute has either primary or secondary stress; the pattern is fixed for compounds with unequal number of constituents in head and attribute—((ÁBC)D) and (A(B̀CD))—but varies when head and attribute each have two. As stated earlier, the reason(s) for the two variants is obscure.

In addition to compounds which belong to the class of nouns, verbs, or adjectives, combinations of morphemes from other word classes, especially determiners, adverbs, and prepositions, are also joined into larger units, often called 'Zusammenrückungen' in German. These can be grouped according to the placement of stress on the first constituent or the last.

(1) There is initial stress on demonstratives and indefinite pronouns, e.g. *dérart, dérgestalt, dérmaßen, jéderzeit, díesmal, mánchmal, éinmal, jédermann, jédesmal, jédweder, kéinmal, níemand, démgemäß,* etc.

(2) Final stress occurs in prepositional 'Zusammenrückungen' regardless of the position of the preposition, e.g. *bergáb, bergáuf, berghináb, kopfúnter, schrägúber, zwischendúrch, mitúnter, anbéi, zuvór,* etc., and *anstátt, beiséite, nachdém, imstánde, zugúnsten, zuwéilen, vorhánden, umsónst, mitníchten, zuínnerst, zunǎchst, durcheinánder, übereinánder, nebeneinánder,* etc. Some of this group also serve as multiple prefixes to verbs, as noted earlier, e.g. *instándsetzen, hervórsprudeln, überéinstimmen,* etc.

10.2 Sentence accent. Under the heading 'word stress', we found a number of regularities for assigning prominence to one syllable of the word. In this book the term 'stress' is used to refer to that syllable of an isolated word which is given the most 'weight' by the speaker and heard by the listener as the most prominent, that syllable marked in an ordinary dictionary.

But speech does not consist of joining isolated words one to another, since the utterances of language are in some sense processed as wholes in the brain. Thought is nonlinear, but speech, since it occurs in time, is linear. In a stretch of speech, such as a sentence, some syllables are heard as more prominent than others. And in any given utterance there is at least one syllable perceived as the most salient. This peak of prominence will be referred to as SENTENCE ACCENT. Sentence accent coincides with the stress of a given word. In the sentence

In der Netzwarte wird rund um die Uhr im Achtstundendienst gearbeitet,

each of the words *Nétzwarte, Achtstúndendienst,* and *geárbeitet* has the stress pattern as marked when uttered in isolation. But in the sentence, the stressed syllable of *Achtstúndendienst* is accorded the greatest prominence of all. It is not only the case that it is pronounced with greater force, but the intonation pattern, the rise and fall of the pitch on it, and the somewhat lengthened syllable (*-stun-*) contribute to its prominence.

Whereas stress rules, although complex, can be formulated for the words constituting the lexicon of German, it is impossible to formulate rules for the accent of entire sentences without taking into account the context of the utterance: what was said previously, the presuppositions about the shared knowledge of speaker and hearer, and the intent of the speaker (to instruct, cajole, be ironic, threaten, express fear, joy, etc.). Sentence accent is discussed further in connection with intonation in section 10.3.

10.3 Intonation. In the following exchange, the question and answer are characterized by a rising and falling of the pitch.

-Wie ist das Wetter heute?
-Sonnig.

In layman's terms, the utterances are said to have a melody; the 'voice' is characterized by rises and falls. *Sonnig* in the foregoing exchange has the pattern high pitch to low pitch. This change in pitch in the course of an utterance is known as INTONATION. That intonation consists of the rises and falls of pitch can be confirmed by simply humming the melody of a sentence, or by picking out the corresponding notes on a musical instrument. This high-to-low pattern, which is often called an INTONATION CONTOUR, is so common that we rarely notice it unless the speaker departs from it, for example, by employing a monotone. The neutral or matter-of-fact answer to the foregoing question has an expected pattern of high-to-low pitch. Since the intonation contour is superimposed, as it were, over the segmental (i.e. the individual) phonemes, intonation is often referred to as SUPRASEGMENTAL.

Several transcriptional systems have been devised to represent the facts of intonation. One can position the syllables on the page according to relative pitch height, e.g.

son-
    nig

or with a series of dashes:

sonnig

or with a continuous line:
    Heute wird es sonnig.

Here the second alternative is adopted: each dash represents a single syllable which is higher, lower or at the same level as the preceding and following syllables. The vertical distance between the dashes represents the relative difference in pitch between two adjacent syllables. The greater the distance between two adjacent dashes, the greater the pitch change. This transcriptional system should not obscure the fact, however, that intonation is normally continuous over a number of syllables. Hence the notion of 'speech melody' is not an inappropriate characterization.

When the answer to the example question is made somewhat longer, the intonation pattern can be transcribed as follows:

(1) Heute ist es sonnig.   - - - -

There is usually some slight pitch change in the early part of the utterance, but we ignore this fact for the time being. The same pattern of high-to-low occurs on the word *sonnig* as when the word stands alone. There is a rise in pitch after *es* to a peak, and then the pitch falls to its lowest point in the whole utterance, signaling to the listener that the utterance is completed.

Where the pitch rises to its highest point is perceptually the most salient part of the utterance for the listener. Experiments show that this fact is primarily due to the abrupt change in pitch, but at least two other factors contribute to the prominence of this stretch of speech: the emphasis on *son-* (sentence accent) and its length. That is, the factors of loudness and duration also contribute to the listener's perception that this syllable, often referred to as the NUCLEAR SYLLABLE, is highlighted above all the rest. The major pitch change typically occurs toward the end of the utterance. Note the following intonation patterns where sentence accent is marked ¦.

(2) Warum bringst du Blúmen mit?   - ‾ ‾ ‾ ¦
                                              -

(3) Wird es morgen sónnig?   - - ‾ ‾ ¦
                                        ‾
(4) Kannst du diese einfache Frage nicht beántworten?

          ¦ ‾
    - - - - - -   - - - - ‾
  -        - - -   - -

Sentence (2), like (1) earlier, ends with a falling pitch after a rise to the nuclear syllable. Sentences (3) and (4) end on a rising pitch. In all four sentences there is a sharp change in pitch adjacent to the nuclear syllable. Rising and falling pitch, as illustrated by these four sentences, represents two patterns of statistically very high occurrence in German.

It is obvious from these examples that the direction of the pitch at the nucleus cannot be correlated with particular sentence types, such as statement and question. Sentences (2) and (3) are both questions, yet each has a different intonation contour. In fact, the patterns of the two could be reversed:

(2a) Warúm bringst du Blumen mit?   - ¦ - - - - ‾

This would be usual if the speaker is asking for a repetition of a previous statement.

                                              ¦
(3a) Wird es morgen sonnig?   - - ‾ -
                                          -

This might be used if the speaker has been asked to repeat a previous question.

Next to rise and fall, a third intonation pattern consists of the pitch remaining more or less the same. This 'sustain' pattern is heard at the end of an incomplete utterance, or in utterances where the speaker expects the listener to complete the sentence, as in (5):

(5) Wenn sie wirklich kommt   - - - - ⁻

or

or when answering a knock at the door:

(6) Ja ⁻

Isolated sentences such as the foregoing can obscure the fact that prosody—intonation, sentence accent, duration, as well as tempo and pause—is closely linked to nonlinguistic factors, especially the situation. By 'situation' is meant the relationship between speaker and hearer, their shared knowledge, the social setting, and the disposition or mood of the speaker. When a sentence such as (2a), for example, is heard in isolation, one is not always certain whether the speaker is merely asking the listener to repeat a statement he/she did not hear, or whether the intent is to express incredulity. The prosodic features of utterances play a significant role in our interpreting the speaker's attitude, but in addition, previous linguistic context, the social context, and the meaning of the utterance all make a contribution as well. Hence it would be a rather questionable task to try to correlate particular intonation patterns with particular speaker attitudes. Discussion here, then, is limited to a brief linguistic description of intonation, with only occasional comments on possible extralinguistic meaning.

Within the basic nuclear rise and nuclear fall patterns, subsets can be distinguished, depending on the position of the prenuclear syllable.

(3) Wird es morgen sonnig?   - - ⁻ ⁻ ⁻

(3b) Wird es morgen sonnig?   - - ⁻ ⁻

The greater distance, i.e. the greater rise in pitch, in (3b) may be used to express surprise. The proviso 'may be' is necessary, since surprise could also be rendered by (3). The greater rise in (3b) is due to a greater fall from the prenuclear syllable.

Pitch fall can also vary from the prenuclear syllable. It rises in:

(1) Heute ist es sonnig.   - - - - ⁻

and falls in:

(7) Heute kommt der Pfarrer.

The latter intonation could be used when the speaker expresses apathy or aversion. The pattern in sentence (1) could also be changed so that the fall from the nuclear syllable is greater than shown. Such a fall would be a common way to express enthusiasm.

It is not the purpose here to construct a complete catalogue of every possible intonation contour and its possible emotional connotations. There is some disagreement on just how many basic contour patterns there are, and which speaker attitudes are expressed by which contours. A few hints on further reading can be found at the end of the chapter.

10.3.1 The tone group. All of the foregoing examples have a single nuclear syllable. But more than one is possible, especially in longer sentences, for example, in (8), where the || indicates the boundary between two tone groups.

(8) Setzt er keine Brille auf, kann er gar nichts sehen.

A tone group is an informational unit dominated by one nuclear syllable. They may, but do not necessarily, coincide with syntactic divisions such as the seam between the two clauses in sentence (8). Compare the following three sentences, where at least three different patterns are possible. In (9), the entire sentence is a single tone group.

(9) Wenn das nicht stimmt, müssen wir von vorne anfangen.

The same sentence can be divided into two tone groups as (9a) shows, where ⟍ indicates a falling pitch on a single syllable.

(9a) Wenn das nicht stimmt, müssen wir von vorne anfangen.

A second possibility for two tone groups is given in (9b), and finally, three tone groups are shown in (9c).

(9b) Wenn das nicht stimmt, müssen wir von vorne anfangen.

(9c) Wenn dás nicht stimmt, müssen wir von vórne anfangen.

There are no formal procedures for analyzing the intonation contour into tone groups. Much depends on the context and the informational content which the speaker wishes to communicate. In example (9c), the higher pitch and accent on *das* clearly has either a contrastive or an emphatic purpose (cf. 10.3.2, 10.3.3) which, apart from the nature of the word itself, presupposes some context.

10.3.2 Contrastive accent. As noted so far, at least one syllable in an utterance receives sentence accent. In isolated sentences, it occurs close to the end, since that is usually where the new information is located, and it is the new information one wants to highlight. In the following sentences, for example, prominence occurs on the last stressed syllable of the noun phrase (the portion of the sentence set in italic type).

(10) Sie wollten *einen guten Eindruck* machen.
(11) Heute haben wir *einige neue Bücher* bekommen.

With no context, the accented syllable is the last stressable one of the noun phrase. The accent is also placed there when *einen guten Eindruck* and *einige neue Bücher* are new information in the context in which they appear. But accent can also fall elsewhere.

(10a) Sie wollten einen gúten Eindruck machen.
(11a) Heute haben wir einige néue Bücher bekommen.

Here the accent is only appropriate if *Eindruck* and *Bücher* are already in the context, either (a) by previous mention, or (b) by mutual understanding between speaker and hearer. In these examples the accent has a contrastive function and is sometimes referred to as CONTRASTIVE ACCENT (as over against the unmarked accent of sentences (10) and (11), where UNMARKED refers to the accent pattern when the sentence is spoken in isolation or without any special contextual condition). In fact, no other pattern is possible when *Eindruck* and *Bücher* are already present in the context as defined. Note that contrast need not refer to previous mention of a particular word, say *schlecht* or *alt,* respectively. Sentence (10a), for instance, could be part of an unfavorable response to an action.

(12) Laß doch diesen Unfug! Wir wollen doch einen gúten Eindruck machen.

10.3.3 Emphatic accent. Alongside unmarked and contrastive accent, a third type can be isolated, EMPHATIC ACCENT. It is possible, for example, to accent every stressable syllable in an utterance in emphatic speech, as in (13a), or most of the syllables, as in (13b).

(13a) Dás wíll ìch nícht! ᵗ ⁱ ⁱ ᵗ

(13b) Das wíll ìch nícht! - ⁱ ⁱ ᵗ

Emphatic accent does not arise from the conditions for unmarked or contrastive accent. It is virtually the equivalent of pronouncing individual words in isolation, except that the pitch pattern is maintained over the whole utterance.

10.4 Rhythm, pause, and tempo. Many linguists include under the heading 'prosody' the phenomena of rhythm, pause, and tempo. Rhythm is related to the alternation of stressed and unstressed syllables, a topic that is not pursued here. Pause refers to breaks in the stream of speech sounds, and tempo to the relative speed of speech. Pause is not susceptible to classification, although it clearly plays a part in the communicative role of speech. Whether and where pauses occur in utterances is largely idiosyncratic. Style of speech is also a factor. Formal speech, for example, tends to be punctuated by more pauses at natural breaks in the sentence, such as at the end of phrases and clauses. Frequent pausing can lend an air of solemnity to a speech. Compare, for instance, the following two versions of the same sentence, where pause is marked with a double slash:

(14a) Eine relative Stabilität in beiden Lagern ist die Voraussetzung dafür//daß die Ost-West-Entspannung in Europa funktionieren kann.
(14b) Eine relative Stabilität in beiden Lagern//ist die Voraussetzung dafür//daß die Ost-West-Entspannung in Europa//funktionieren kann.

The latter version (14b) could be characterized as more formal, as the speaker's pauses make the sentence sound 'weightier'. Style, as well as length of utterance, may dictate certain breaks. Pause may also be used to effect surprise, as when it is placed before a final *nicht*.

(15) Am folgenden Tag unterschrieb der Gesandte den Vertrag// nicht.

The reading of prepared texts differs from spontaneous speech. In the former, the occurrence of pauses at the end of grammatical units such as phrases may be more likely, but even then, the reading of a text is subject to speaker interpretation. In normal, unrehearsed speech, pauses can occur when the speaker hesitates, stops and starts over, or wishes to render a message more emphatic by employing pause, as shown in (16).

(16) Du//und kein anderer//Nur//du.

Tempo, of course, has to do with the relative rapidity of speech, a topic touched on in the following chapter. It is clearly a matter of speaker idiosyncracy as well as emotional state. Characteristics of the speech signal, such as pause and tempo, which are not subject to formalization by rules, are often termed PARALINGUISTIC.

Further reading

There are literally hundreds of books and articles on various aspects of German prosody. For the beginner, however, most treatments of the subject are simply too demanding. Covering some of the same ground in this chapter in brief scope are Chapters 2, 3 and 4 in:

MacCarthy, Peter. 1975. Pronunciation of German. London: Oxford University Press.

Four book-length studies can be recommended for the more linguistically advanced student:

Essen, Otto von. 1964. Grundzüge der hochdeutschen Satzintonation 2. Aufl. Ratingen: A. Henn.
Isačenko, Alexander, and Hans-Joachim Schädlich. 1970. A model of Standard German intonation. The Hague: Mouton. (Janua linguarum, series practica, 113).
Pheby, John. 1975. Intonation und Grammatik im Deutschen. Berlin: Akadmie-Verlag.
Stock, Eberhard, and Christina Zacharias. 1973. Deutsche Satzintonation. Leipzig: VEB Bibliographisches Institut. (Written for foreign learners of German; keyed to an accompanying record.)

Approximately half of:

Stötzer, Ursula. 1975. Deutsche Aussprache. Leipzig: VEB Verlag Enzyklopädie,

is devoted to questions of accent.
Some helpful general studies on prosody include:

Ladefoged, Peter. 1975. A course in phonetics. Chapter 10. New York: Harcourt Brace Jovanovich. (2nd ed., 1982.)
Lehiste, Ilse. 1970. Suprasegmentals. Cambridge, Mass.: MIT Press.

Problems

Problem 1. Indicate which syllable receives primary stress.
(1) beängstigend
(2) übervorteilen
(3) herumspazieren

(4) abmarschieren
(5) vorenthalten
(6) bevormunden
(7) entlanggehen
(8) entgegentreten
(9) zuvorkommen
(10) mißgefallen

Problem 2. Indicate by use of the dash notation the intonation of the second of each of the following exchanges. The syllable bearing the sentence accent is marked in each case.

(1) -Wo ist denn deine Karte?   - ᵎ - - - -
    -Weiß ich nicht.

(2) -Da kommt er schon.   - ᵎ -
    -Ich sehe gar nichts.

(3) -Willst du mit?   - - ᵎ
    -Ich habe jetzt keine Zeit.

(4) -Ich habe kein Geld bei mir.   - - - - ᵎ -
    -Und ich soll dir was leihen?

(5) -Beeile dich!   - ᵎ -

    -Steh doch mal still!

Problem 3. Divide the following three-member compounds into attribute and head—either ((AB)(C)) or ((A)(BC))—and indicate where primary stress occurs.
(1) Wohnbauförderung
(2) Winterfahrplan
(3) Sozialarbeiterteam
(4) Krankenhausaufenthalt
(5) Forschungsschwerpunkt
(6) Einparteiherrschaft
(7) Baumwollindustrie
(8) Lebensmittelladen
(9) Zehnklassenschule
(10) Wohnungsbauprogramm

Problem 4. Divide the following four-member compounds into attribute and head—((A)(BCD)) or ((ABC)(D))—and indicate where primary stress occurs.
(1) Kernkraftwerkunfall
(2) Zuckerrohranbaugebiet
(3) Mammut-Wasserkraftwerk
(4) Kupfer-Bergbaureserven

(5) Fallschirmjägergeneral
(6) Hochschulstatistikgesetz
(7) Kulturpreisträgeraesthetik
(8) Schießbudenfigurvorlage
(9) Weihnachtsbaumsatz
(10) Wohnraumbeschaffungsprogramm
(11) Mittagsrückfahrkarte
(12) Kommerzfernsehanhänger

Problem 5. In the section on word stress, two generalizations were made regarding multiple prefixes: (1) when stressable and unstressable prefixes occur together, the stress falls on the former, e.g. *úmbenennen, bevórmunden;* and (2) when two stressable prefixes occur, the stress falls on the second, e.g. *voránkommen.* Reformulate these facts in a single succinct rule.

> Phonemes must not be thought of as building blocks from which individual words are put together. Rather, every word is a phonetic whole, a 'gestalt', and which is recognized by the listener as a gestalt, just as a familiar person is recognized on the street by his form as a whole.
>
> —*N. I. Trubetzkoy*

Chapter 11
Sentence phonetics

11.0 Tempo and style. In earlier chapters, phonetics and phonology were discussed in terms of individual sounds and isolated words in careful speech. In actual speech, however, words are not pronounced in isolation, but are constituents of larger wholes—phrases, sentences and texts—where the complex interaction of breathing, voicing, and movement of the articulating organs is centrally controlled by the brain.

The isolated speech sound is a necessary construct of linguistic analysis, but sounds rarely occur in isolation. In the context of normal speaking, the phonetic realization of an underlying phoneme is conditioned by: (1) its relative position in the word; (2) the rapidity of speech; and (3) the style of speaking, something which is related to the social context.

The first condition was discussed earlier in Chapter 6. There the phonetic realization of phonemes in the individual word was treated. In the present chapter, the focus is on conditions (2) and (3): what happens to speech sounds when the speed and style of speaking vary?

Speech tempo and speech style are simultaneously active in the realization of the underlying phonological representation of longer utterances—phrases, sentences, and texts. Both concepts are difficult to quantify in precise terms. Rapidity is clearly a scalar notion: a given sentence may be spoken at an increasingly rapid rate from very slow to extremely fast. For our purposes, we distinguish only between 'slow' and 'rapid'. Often the musical terms 'lento' and 'presto' (or 'allegro'), respectively, are used.

In like manner, two styles are distinguished: formal and informal, each of which is a function of a social context. Formal style is usual in lectures, sermons, and the reading aloud of literary texts, as well as in broadcasting. Informal style is usual in round-table discussions and in casual conversation among friends and family, the first situation being slightly more formal than the latter. Clearly, degree of acquaintanceship among the speech partners, the familiarity of the topic or topics of discussion, as well as other more individual and personal factors, play a role in assessing the degree of formality and hence the style of speaking used. Furthermore, speed and style are clearly simultaneous factors; speed can vary from participant to participant and even within the same individual's speech from one phrase to the next, depending on the importance which the individual attaches to his message, difficulties in formulating thoughts, etc. These variables make a systematic classification of phonetic 'outputs' more difficult, but not impossible. Certain phenomena occur with such regularity that their systematic assignment to factors of speed and style can hardly be overlooked. The effect of these factors is examined by considering two texts—one, the transcription of a speech read at moderate speed, the other a conversation, where both lento and presto forms are transcribed.

11.1 A text in formal style. The first text is an excerpt from a speech about Thomas Mann on the occasion of the hundredth anniversary of his birth. Each line of the speech is followed by four transcriptions (a) to (d).

The (a) lines represent a phonetic transcription of the speech. The (b) lines indicate possible alternative pronunciations of certain words and phrases. In the (a) or the (b) line a double diagonal line or double slash (//) in the transcription indicates a pause. Spacing between the 'words' in the phonetic transcription is merely for ease of reading and does not represent anything in speech.

The (c) lines present a word-for-word literal translation of each line of the German text. Where a hyphen appears between two forms, e.g. Text I, (1c) 'of-his', two English words correspond to one word in the German, in this instance, *seines*. Where more than one German word corresponds to one English word, the German words are given immediately following the English word, e.g. Text I, (5c) *justification=(Fug und Recht)*. Where no translation is possible, the German word in parentheses and in italic type occurs in its ordered position within the string of English words, e.g. Text II, (6c): *recall (sich)* . . . Otherwise, the number of English words in each (c) line matches exactly the number of German words. The (d) lines present an idiomatic English translation of the German text.

I. Formal style

(1)   Thomas Mann verbrachte die Hälfte seines Lebens, das
(1a) [tʰoːmas man fɛɐ̯bʀaxtə di hɛlftə zaɪ̯nəs leːbəns das
(1b)   leːbm̩s
(1c) Thomas Mann spent the half of-his life, the
(1d) Thomas Mann spent half of his life, the

(2)   zweite und das dritte Viertel, von 1894
(2a) tsʏ̯aɪ̯tə ʔʊnt das d̥ʀɪtə fɪɐ̯tl̩ fɔn ʔaxtseːnhʊndɐtfɪɐ̯ʊntnɔʏ̯ntsɪç
(2b)

(2c) second and the third quarter, from 1894
(2d) second and third quarters of it, from 1894

(3) bis 1933 in München,
(3a) bɪs nɔÿntseːnhʊndɐtdʀaɪʊntdʀaɪsɪç ʔɪn mʏnçɛn
(3b)   mʏnçən
(3c) to 1933 in Munich,
(3d) to 1933, in Munich,

(4) aber er sprach von München nie als von seiner Heimat-
(4a) ʔaːbɐ ʔeɐ ʃpʀaːx fɔn mʏnçɛn niː ʔals fɔn zaɪnɐ haɪmaːt
(4b)
(4c) but he spoke about Munich never as about his home-
(4d) but he never spoke of Munich as being his home

(5) stadt; natürlich nicht, das können mit Fug und Recht
(5a) ʃtatʰ natʰyɐlɪç nɪçtʰ das kʰœnən mɪt fuːk ʔʊnt ʀɛçt
(5b)
(5c) town; of-course not; that can with justification = (*Fug und Recht*)
(5d) town. Understandably so, since only very few people

(6) ja nur die allerwenigsten, und sie repräsentieren unsere
(6a) ja nuɐ di ʔalɐveːnɪçstən ʔʊnt zˌiː ʀɛpʀɛzɛntʰiːʀən ʔʊnzəʀə
(6b)   ɣɛpɣɛzɛntʰiːɣn̩
(6c) indeed only the very-fewest, and they represent our
(6d) can do that, after all, with any justification, and these do

(7) Stadt durchaus nicht immer auf die gewinnendste Weise.
(7a) ʃtat dʊɐçʔaʊs nɪçt ʔɪmɐ ʔaʊf di gəvɪnəntstə vaɪzə
(7b)
(7c) city absolutely not always in the most-appealing manner.
(7d) not always represent our city in the most appealing manner.

(8) Thomas Mann nannte München durch vierzig Jahre,
(8a) tʰoːmas man nantə mʏnçɛn dʊɐç fiɐtsɪç jaːʀə
(8b)
(8c) Thomas Mann called Munich through forty years
(8d) For forty years, Thomas Mann always referred modestly

(9) stets bescheidentlich »die Stadt, in der ich lebe«.
(9a) ʃteːts bəʃaɪdn̩tlɪç di ʃtat ʔɪn deɐ ʔɪç leːbə
(9b)
(9c) always modestly 'the city in which I live'.
(9d) to Munich as 'the city where I live'.

(10) Aber er verstand sich als einen Münchner, das doch und
(10a) ʔaːbɐ ʔeɐ fɛɐʃtant zˌɪç ʔals ʔaɪnən mʏnçnɐ das dˌɔx ʔʊnt
(10b)

(10c) But he understood himself as a Munich-citizen, that indeed and
(10d) But he most certainly understood himself to be a citizen

(11) ganz gewiß. Denn unter einem Münchner, so sagte er in
(11a) g̊ants g̊əvɪs dɛn ʔʊntɐ ʔaɪ̯nəm mʏnçnɐ zo zɑːktə ʔeɐ̯ ʔɪn
(11b)
(11c) quite certainly. For by a Munich-citizen, so said he in
(11d) of Munich; of that there is no doubt. For as he said in

(12) seiner Rede zur Eröffnung der Münchner Gesellschaft
(12a) zaɪnɐ ʁeːdə tsuɐ̯ ʔɛɐ̯ʔœfnʊŋ deɐ̯ mʏnçnɐ g̊əzɛlʃaft
(12b)   ɣeːdə
(12c) his speech at-the opening of-the Munich Society
(12d) his speech at the opening of the Munich Society

(13) 1926, verstehe man nicht etwa nur einen in
(13a) nɔÿntseːnhʊndɐtz̊ɛksʊntsy̨antsɪç fɛɐ̯ʃteːə man nɪçt ʔety̨a
(13b)
(13c) 1926, understands one not, say, only someone in
(13d) in 1926, one is not just a citizen

(14) München Geborenen, sondern alle, die durch Leben und
(14a) nuɐ ʔaɪ̯nən ʔɪn mʏnçɛn g̊əboːʁənən zɔndɐn ʔalə di dʊɐ̯ç leːbən
(14b)   g̊əboːɐ̯nən   leːbm̩
(14c) Munich born, but all who by life and
(14d) of Munich by birth, but by virtue of being tied to the

(15) Wirken mit München verknüpft sind und denen
(15a) ʔʊnt vɪɐ̯kən mɪt mʏnçɛn fɛɐ̯knypft z̊ɪnt ʔʊnt d̊enən
(15b)   vɪɐ̯kn̩
(15c) work with Munich connected are and for-whom
(15d) city by life and work, and by having

(16) Ansehung und Geltung der Stadt am Herzen liegt. Wenn
(16a) ʔanzeːʊŋ ʔʊnt g̊ɛltʊŋ deɐ̯ ʃtat ʔam hɛɐ̯tsn̩ liːktʰ vɛn
(16b)
(16c) standing and importance of-the city on-the heart lies. If
(16d) the standing and the importance of the city close to one's

(17) Sie - nämlich seine damaligen Zuhörer - diese Ansicht
(17a) ziː nɛːmlɪç zaɪ̯nə daːmalɪgən tsuːhøːʁɐ dizə ʔanzɪçt
(17b)
(17c) you—namely, his then hearers—this view
(17d) heart. If you, he said, referring to his listeners then,

(18) teilen, und ich glaube, die meisten von Ihnen haben
(18a) tʰaɪ̯lən ʔʊnt ɪç g̊laʊ̯bə di maɪ̯stən fɔn ʔinən haːbən
(18b)   maɪ̯stn̩   haːbm̩

(18c) share, and I believe the most of you have
(18d) share this view, and I think most of you have

(19)   Grund dazu (das war in München immer so), so werden
(19a) gʀʊnt d̥atsu: das ɣaɐ̯ ʔɪn mʏnçɛn ʔɪmɐ̯ zo: zo vɛɐ̯d̥ən
(19b)
(19c) reason to (that was in Munich always so), then will
(19d) reason to (that was always the case in Munich), then you

(20)   Sie nicht weiter Anstoß daran nehmen, daß ich, der
(20a) zi nɪçt vaɪ̯tɐ ʔanʃto:s d̥aʀan ne:mən das ʔɪc deɐ̯
(20b)
(20c) you not further offense to-it take, that I, who
(20d) will not take offense if I, though

(21)   ich ja nicht gerade ein Saupreiß, aber doch ein
(21a) ɪç j̊a nɪçt g̊əʀa:d̥ə ʔaɪn zaʊ̯pʰʀaɪs ʔabɐ dɔx ʔaɪn
(21b)   g̊əɣa:d̥ə
(21c) I indeed not exactly a Prussian, but still an
(21d) not exactly a Prussian, but

(22)   unverleugneter Norddeutscher bin, bei dieser Gelegenheit
(22a) ʔʊnfɛɐ̯lɔɥgnətɐ nɔɐ̯td̥ɔɥtʃɐ bɪn baɪ̯ dizɐ gəle:gənhaɪ̯t
(22b)
(22c) undeniable North-German am, on this occasion
(22d) undeniably a North German,

(23)   das Wort nehme.
(23a) d̥as ɣɔɐ̯t ne:mə]
(23b)
(23c) the word take.
(23d) hold forth on this occasion.

(From: Peter de Mendelssohn, 'Ein Schriftsteller in München', in *Thomas Mann 1875-1975*. Vorträge in München-Zürich-Lübeck. Hrsg. von Beatrix Bludau, Eckhard Heftrich und Helmut Koopmann. Frankfurt:S. Fischer, 1977, p. 15; cited by permission of the publisher. The original text is not phonetically transcribed).

11.2 Discussion. The transcription of this speech shows a number of regular differences from the expected phonetic output of single, isolated words, differences which can be subsumed under the headings 'loss' and 'assimilation'. A third category encompasses the reduction of so-called 'weak forms', short, mainly grammatical morphemes, such as articles and pronouns, which regularly occur unstressed.

11.2.1 Loss. This heading includes elision, that is, the nonrealization of a segment, as well as the lessening of articulatory precision.

(a) Loss of /ə/ before nasal and lateral is, of course, obligatory when a fricative precedes, e.g. final /-ən/ in *Herzen* [hɛɐ̯tsn̩] (line 16, Text I; cf. Table 6.1). It is somewhat less common after stops except in presto speech, e.g. *bescheidentlich* [bəʃaɪdn̩tlɪç]. After sonorants—both consonantal and vocalic—it is rarer; cf., for example, the full /ə/ finally in *einen* [ʔaɪnən] (line 10) and *teilen* [tʰaɪlən] (line 17), except after stressed syllables, when followed by another /-ə/, e.g. *geborenen* [gəboːɐ̯nən] (line 14b).

(b) Loss of /t/ in obstruent clusters. In formal texts this loss is not as pronounced as in informal ones. In Text I, /t/ is lost before /ts/ in *achtzehn* /axttseːn/ [ʔaxtseːn] (line 2).

(c) Centralizing of vowels. In most cases it is a question of tense or peripheral vowels losing their tenseness and becoming lax, i.e. more centralized or nonperipheral (cf. Figure 2.5). In Text I, this occurs in *repräsentieren* (compare line 6b with 6a). In the diminutive suffix *-chen* (line 3b), the underlying lax vowel /ɛ/ may be completely centralized to [ə] in presto speech, or may even elide entirely, resulting in [-çn].

11.2.2 Assimilation. Assimilation occurs when two segments become more like one another in one or more features. In Text I, all assimilatory phenomena involve adjacent segments and in every case assimilation moves from left to right ('progressive assimilation'); the later segment is assimilated to the earlier, for example, in the presto form *leben(s)* [leːbm̩s] (lines 1b and 14b) and *wirken* [vɪɐ̯kŋ̍] (line 15b); the nasal following the stop is assimilated to it in point of articulation (HOMORGANIC ASSIMILATION).

11.2.3 Weak forms. Certain classes of morphemes—especially pronouns, articles, prepositions, conjunctions, and some adverbs—tend to be unaccented in speech (hence 'weak'), unless they occur in emphatic or contrastive contexts (cf. Chapter 10 on emphatic and contrastive accent). Lack of stress means that tense vowels and /ɑː/ are realized short. There are several such examples in Text I, e.g.:

die	[di]	(lines 1, 7, 9)
er	[ʔeɐ̯]	(lines 4, 10)
nur	[nuɐ̯]	(line 6)
der	[deɐ̯]	(line 9)
zur	[tsuɐ̯]	(line 12)
aber	[ʔabɐ]	(line 21)

In lines 6 and 17, *sie* /ziː/ occurs in a position of stress and hence is long; compare line 20, where *Sie* occurs in unstressed position. In line 19, /zoː/ occurs in both accented and unaccented position, hence the two realizations [zoː] and [zo].

Although the weak forms here could easily be subsumed under the heading 'loss', their unique behavior in informal speech requires their being treated as a distinct group.

All three of these categories—loss, assimilation and weak forms—can be treated under the general heading 'reduction'. Assimilation means a reduction in the difference between two segments; in more rapid speech, total assimilation may occur, where the differences are completely abolished (cf. the discussion of Text II). Loss, on the other hand, may mean elision, the omission of an entire segment, or it may mean loss of articulatory precision, such as the tendency of peripheral vowels to move toward the center of the vowel space (cf. Chapter 6, Problem 8). Reduction in weak forms means the loss of length in tense vowels, as well as other reductions to be discussed later. Even in the articulation of isolated words, the organs do not assume a discrete position for each individual sound. While in the process of articulation of one sound, the organs are already moving toward the production of the next, or even more distant ones. The more rapid the speech, the less time there is for the articulators to move into position. Moreover, differences exist in the speed with which the various articulators move. For example, in the presto forms of *Leben* (line 1b) and *Wirken* (line 15b), the velum is lowered for the articulation of the nasal /n/, but the lips and dorsovelar contact, respectively, do not move simultaneously, resulting in each case in a homorganic nasal, [m] ([leːbm̩]) and [ŋ] ([vɪ̞ɐ̯kŋ̩]), respectively (homorganic = having the same point of articulation).

11.3 A text in informal style. Reduction phenomena occur with greater frequency and with greater informality in presto speech. In Text II, the same procedure is followed as for Text I. The full transcription of lento speech is given in the (a)-lines; the (b)-lines give the pronunciation of presto speech. Not all the possible reductions are recorded, and, in general, once a presto form is given, it is not repeated later in the transcription.

The context is a conversation in an art shop. Herr Ahrens, a frequent customer, enters with a package under his arm, a print to be framed (referred to in line 9 as *Ihre Sachen*). The major part of the dialogue concerns an original of a print by the artist, Max Ernst, of which Ahrens has a sample copy (referred to as *diesen Max Ernst* in line 4).

Text II. Informal style

(1) *Ahrens*: Tag, Herr Schumann
(1a)   [tʰɑːk hɛɐ̯ ʃuːman
(1b)
(1c) Hello, Mr. Schumann.
(1d) Hello, Mr. Schumann.

(2) *Schumann*: Tag, Herr Ahrens. Haben Sie mal wieder was
(2a)   tʰɑːk hɛɐ̯ ɑːɐ̯ns   haːbm̩ zi mal vidɐ vas
(2b)   haːm zi (zə)

(2c) Hello, Mr. Ahrens. Have you once again something
(2d) Hello, Mr. Ahrens. Have you purchased anything

(3) erstanden?
(3a) ɐ̯ʃtandn̩
(3b) ɛʃtann̩
(3c) purchased?
(3d) again?

(4) *A*: Ja und nein. Es ist so: erstmal bin ich noch in
(4a) ja ʊn naɪ̯n ʔɛs ɪsːo: ʔɐ̯ʃtmal bɪn ɪç nɔx ɪn
(4b)   nɔxn̩
(4c) Yes and no. It is thus: first am I still in
(4d) Yes and no. The thing is this: first of all, I'm

(5) Ihrer Schuld. Sie hatten mir mal diesen Max Ernst
(5a) iːɐ̯ ʃʊlt zi hatn̩ mɪɐ̯ mal dizn̩ maks ʔɛɐ̯nst
(5b) ɪɐ̯   haʔn̩ mɐ̯
(5c) your debt. You had to-me once this Max Ernst
(5d) still indebted to you. You once gave me this Max Ernst

(6) da mitgegeben. Sie entsinnen sich ...
(6a) d̥a mɪtg̊əge:bm̩   zi ɛntz̩ɪnn̩ zɪç
(6b) ð̥a mɪtg̊əge:bm̩   ɛnzɪnn̩
(6c) here given-to-take-with. You recall (*sich*) ...
(6d) here to take along with me. You recall ...

(7) *S*: Ja, ich habe das Blatt, wollen Sie es mal sehen?
(7a) ja çhap d̥as b̥lat   vɔln̩ zi əs mal ze:n
(7b)   zis
(7c) Yes, I have the print. Want you it just to-see?
(7d) Yes, I have the print. Do you want to take a look at it?

(8) *A*: Das ist ja schön. Ja, ich würde es gern mal sehen.
(8a) das ɪs ja ʃøː:n   jɑ: çyyrts g̊ɛɐ̯n mal ze:n
(8b)   ma
(8c) This is really nice. Yes, I would it gladly just see.
(8d) That'd be really nice. Yes, I'd very much like to see it.

(9) *S*: Wollen wir erstmal Ihre Sachen machen oder soll
(9a) vɔln̩ vɪɐ̯ ɐ̯ʃtmal iːɐ̯ zaxn̩ maxn̩ odɐ̯ zɔl
(9b)   vɐ̯ ɐ̯ʃmal ɪɐ̯ə zaxŋ̩ maxŋ̩ ɔdɐ̯ (ɔɾɐ̯)
(9c) Want we first your things do or shall
(9d) Shall we take care of your things first or shall

(10) ich es Ihnen erstmal zeigen?
(10a) ɪçs iːn: ɐ̯ʃtmal tsaɪ̯gŋ̩
(10b)   iːn ɐ̯ʃma tsaɪ̯ŋŋ̩ (tsaɪ̯ŋ)

(10c) I it to-you first show?
(10d) I show it to you first?

(11) *A*: Zeigen wir erstmal das Blatt, [ich] würde doch gern mal
(11a) tsaɪɡn̩ viɐ̯ ɛɐ̯stmal das b̥lat   vʏɐ̯t d̥ɔx g̊ɛɐ̯n mal
(11b)   vɐ ɛɐ̯sma   ma
(11c) Show we first the print. I would just gladly once
(11d) Let's take a look at the print first. I'd just like

(12) sehen, wie das so im Original ausfällt.
(12a) ze:n vi das:o ɪm ɔʏɪɡɪna:l aʊ̯sfɛlt
(12b)   vɪ   m̩ ɔʏɪɡəna:l
(12c) see, how that just in-the original comes-off.
(12d) to see how it comes off in the original.

(13) [Ich] komme eben doch nicht dazu, das zu kaufen. Das
      übersteigt
(13a) kʰɔm ebm̩ dɔx nɪç d̥atsu das tsu kʰaʊ̯fm̩ das yb̥ɐʃtaɪ̯kt
(13b)   emm̩   das:u   kʰaʊ̯fm̩
(13c) I manage simply after-all not to, that to buy. That surpasses
(13d) But I simply can't manage to buy it. It simply goes

(14) doch meine Möglichkeiten, und was hatten Sie gesagt?
(14a) d̥ɔx maɪ̯nə mø:ɡlɪçkaɪ̯tn̩ ʊn vas hatn̩ zi ɡəza:kt
(14b)   haʔn̩
(14c) simply my possibilities. And what had you said?
(14d) beyond my means. And what is it you said then?

(15) 4 700?
(15a) fiɐ̯taʊ̯zn̩tzi:mhʊndɐt
(15b)   hʊnɐt
(15c) 4,700?
(15d) 4,700?

(16) *S*: Nein, 2 950.
(16a) naɪn tsʋaɪ̯taʊ̯zn̩tnɔʏnhʊndɐtfʏmftsɪç
(16b)   tsʋaɪ̯taʊ̯zn̩nɔʏnhʊnɐtfʏŋsɪç
(16c) No. 2,950.
(16d) No. 2,950.

(17) *A*: Ich meine, das ist zwar immer noch eine ganze Menge
(17a) çmaɪ̯nə das ɪs:ʋa: ɪmɐ nɔx nə ɡansə mɛŋə
(17b)
(17c) I think, that is to-be-sure still = (*immer noch*) a whole lot
(17d) I do think that's still a lot of money,

(18) und ist doch ein schönes Blatt.
(18a) ʊn ɪs d̥ɔxn̩ ʃø:nəs b̥lat

(18b)
(18c) and is still a lovely print.
(18d) but it is a lovely print.

(19) *S*: [Es] ist ein schönes Blatt, nicht? Ich hatte es im Rahmen.
(19a) ʔɪsn̩ ʃøːnəs b̥lat   nɪç   çhats ɪm ɣɑːmn̩
(19b)   ne   ɣɑːmm̩
(19c) It is a lovely print, isn't-it? I had it in-a frame.
(19d) It is a lovely print, isn't it? I had it in a frame,

(20) Da muß ich es jetzt auch wieder herein. Den hat
(20a) da mʊs ɪçs j̊ɛts ɑu̯x ɣiːdɐ ɣaɪ̯n   deːn hat
(20b)   mʊz
(20c) So must I it now also again put-in. It has
(20d) and now I'll have to put it in one again. Someone

(21) hier jemand ihn kaputt geschmissen. Da kann ich es
(21a) hiɐ̯ jemant in kapʰʊt g̊əʃmɪsn̩   da kan ɪçs
(21b)
(21c) here someone it to-bits smashed. So can I it
(21d) smashed it to bits here. I'll have to put it back

(22) mal gleich wieder reintun. [Es] wäre fast schon
(22a) mal glaɪ̯ç vidɐ ɣaɪ̯ntuːn   veɣə fast ʃon
(22b)   ʃɔn
(22c) sometime just again put-in. It would-have-been just about
(22d) in one again sometime. It would just about have been

(23) kaputtgegangen.
(23a) kapʰʊtg̊əgaŋn̩
(23b) kapʰʊkg̊əgaŋ̍ŋ (g̊əgaŋ̍)
(23c) ruined.
(23d) ruined.

(24) *A*: Ach so. Haben Sie eventuell noch einen andern
(24a) ʔax z̥o hɑːm zi ɛvɛntu̯ɛl nɔxn̩ andɐn
(24b)   anːɐn
(24c) I see. Have you perhaps yet an other
(24d) I see. Do you perhaps have another interested

(25) Interessenten?
(25a) ɪntəɣɛsɛntn̩
(25b) ɪntəɣəsɛntn̩
(25c) interested-party?
(25d) party?

(26) *S*: Ja und nein. Also, ich habe jemanden, der auch darauf
(26a) ja ʊn naɪ̯n ʔalzo   çhɑːbə jemandn̩ deɐ̯ ɑu̯x dɣau̯f

(26b)   ʔazo
(26c) Yes and no. That-is, I have someone who also about-it
(26d) Yes and no. I mean, I have someone who's also

(27)   reflektiert, aber sonst also einen direkten Kunden, Käufer
(27a) ɣɛflɛktʰiːɐ̯tʰ ʔɑːbɐ̯ zɔns alzo n̩dɪɣɛktn̩ kʰʊndn̩ kʰɔy̆fɐ̯
(27b) ɣəflɛktʰiːɐ̯tʰ ʔaßɐ̯ zɔns azo n̩dəɣɛkɳ̍ kʰʊnn̩
(27c) is-thinking, but otherwise (*also*) an actual customer, buyer
(27d) thinking about it, but an actual customer or buyer,

(28)   habe ich nicht.
(28a) habɪç nɪç
(28b) haßɪç
(28c) have I not.
(28d) no.

(29)   *A*: [Ich] finde es ein sehr schönes Blatt. Ich meine, es
(29a) fɪndəs a̯ɪn zeːɐ̯ ʃøːnəs b̪latʰ   çma̯ɪnə ʔɛs
(29b) fɪnnəs
(29c) I find it a very lovely print. I mean it
(29d) I find it to be a very lovely print. I mean it's

(30)   entspricht seinen letzten Bildern. Auch in diesem Oeuvre-
(30a) ɛntʃpʀɪçt za̯ɪnn̩ lɛtstn̩ bɪldɐn ʔaʊ̯x ɪn dizm̩ øːvɣə
(30b)
(30c) is-in-keeping-with his last pictures. Also in this works
(30d) in keeping with his last pictures. In this catalogue of

(31)   Katalog ist ja ein ähnliches von der Struktur her.
(31a) kataloːk ɪs ja a̯ɪn eːnlɪçəs fɔn dɛɐ̯ ʃtʀʊkʰtʰuɐ̯ hɛɐ̯
(31b)   fn̩ dɐ̯
(31c) catalogue is, you-know = (*ja*) a similar-one from the structure (*her*).
(31d) his works, there's one that's similar from a structural point of view,
       you know.

(32)   Ich könnte das allenfalls über eine längere Ratenzahlung
(32a) çkœntə das aln̩fals   ybɐ̯ nə lɛŋəɣə ɣaːtn̩tsaːluŋ hɪn
(32b)   ybɐ̯ (ɣßɐ̯)
(32c) I could that at-most over a longer installment-payment
(32d) At most I might be able to finance it by installments

(33)   hin finanzieren. Ich habe einfach nicht . . . die 2 950
(33a) fɪnantsiːɣn̩   çhaß a̯ɪnfax nɪç   di tsɣa̯ɪtaʊ̯zn̩tnɔy̆nhʊndɐt
(33b)   tsɣa̯ɪtaʊ̯zn̩nɔy̆nhʊnɐt
(33c) (*hin*) finance. I have simply not . . . the 2,950
(33d) over a longer period. I simply don't have the 2,950

(34)   Mark habe ich nicht parat. Ich wüßte gar nicht,

(34a) fʏmftsɪç maɐ̯k habɪç nɪç paɣaːtʰ çʏ̯ʏstə gɑː nɪç
(34b) fʏm̩sɪç
(34c) marks have I not on-hand. I would-know at-all not
(34d) marks on hand. I wouldn't know at all

(35) wie wir das machen müßten.
(35a) vi vɪɐ̯ das maxn̩ mʏstn̩
(35b) vɐ̯ maxŋ̍
(35c) how we that do might-have-to.
(35d) how we might have to do that.

(36) S: Wenn Sie diese Raten wollten, wäre mir das recht.
(36a) vɛn zi dizə ɣɑːtn̩ vɔltn̩   veːɣə mɪɐ̯ das ɣɐçt
(36b)
(36c) If you these installments would-want, would-be to-me that OK.
(36d) If you would want these installments, that would be OK with me.

(37) A: Ich bin auch gar nicht sicher, ob ich das will. Das
(37a) çb̩ɪn aʊ̯x ɡ̊ɑː nɪç zɪçɐ̯   ɔp ɪç d̥as ʏ̯ɪl   das
(37b)
(37c) I am even at-all not sure whether I that want. That
(37d) I'm not even at all sure whether I want to do that.

(38) ist eben das Problem. Ja, ob ich dafür im Augenblick
(38a) ɪs ebm̩ das pʀɔbleːm   jɑː   ʔɔp ɪç d̥afʏɐ̯ ɪm aʊ̯g̊ŋ̍blɪk
(38b)
(38c) is just the problem. Uh, whether I for-it at-the moment
(38d) That's just the problem. Uh, whether I want to spend

(39) 2 950 Mark ausgeben will . . . da kommen jetzt so andere
(39a) tsʏ̯aɪ̯taʊ̯zn̩tnɔ̈ȳnhʊndɐ̯tfʏmftsɪç maɐ̯k aʊ̯sgebm̩ vɪl   da
(39b)
(39c) 2,950 marks spend want . . . (da) come now (so) other
(39d) 2,950 marks at the moment. There are other priorities

(40) Prioritäten dazu.
(40a) kʰɔmm̩ jɛts z̥o andəɣə pʀɪɔɣɪtɛːtn datsuː]
(40b) kʰɔm   andɣə
(40c) priorities in-addition.
(40d) that have to be considered in addition right now.

(From: Werner Kallmeyer. 'Aushandlung und Bedeutungskonstitution', in *Dialogforschung. Jahrbuch 1980 des Instituts für deutsche Sprache.* Hrsg. von Peter Schröder und Hugo Steger. Düsseldorf:Schwann, 1981, 89-127 (Sprache der Gegenwart Bd. 54), 118-19; used with permission of the publisher. The original text is not phonetically transcribed and has been revised slightly for purposes of the discussion).

11.3.1 Loss.

(a) Loss of /ə/.

(i) Loss of /ə/ before nasal, common in verb and adjective endings, is widespread, and in contrast to formal speech, occurs in all environments, e.g. after stop (*erstanden,* line 3 [ɛɐ̯ʃtandn̩]), after liquid (*wollen,* line 7 [vɔln̩]), after vowel (*sehen,* line 8 [ze:n]), after nasal (*entsinnen,* line 6 [ɛntzɪnn̩]), and after fricative (*Sachen,* line 9 [zaxn̩]).

(ii) Loss of /ə/ as the marker for the first person singular present occurs in Text II in *habe* (line 7 [hap]), *würde* (lines 8, 11 [vʏɐ̯t]), and *komme* (line 13 [kʰɔm]). The only restriction on the loss of this grammatical marker is the prohibition on the occurrence of a final syllabic nasal ([m̩], [n̩], [ŋ̍]); for example, only *trockne ich* and *ich trockne* with final schwa are possible.

(iii) Loss of /ə/ after stressed syllable before following /ə/ occurs once in the text: *andere* ([andɣə]) in line 40b (cf. *geborenen* in Text I, line 14b). Elision in this environment is very common when both schwas precede nasal, e.g. *offenen* [ɔfnən], *geschlossenen* [gəʃlɔsnən]. Elision of the first schwa is obligatory in all styles and tempos of speech in verbs derived from adjectives and nouns, e.g. adj. *trocken,* verb *trockn-en;* noun *Regen,* verb *regn-en* (cf. Chapter 6).

(b) Loss of [ɐ̯]. In informal speech, final [ɐ̯] after [ɑ:] may be elided, e.g. *zwar* (line 17) and *gar* (line 34). The elision results from failure to raise the tongue the short distance from [ɑ:] to [ɐ̯] (cf. Figure 2.5).

(c) Loss of /t/. The articulation of apical consonants requires a rapid and quite precise movement of the tongue in contrast to labial and velar consonants. In rapid speech, this movement is thus frequently omitted when /t/ clusters with other consonants, especially in unstressed positions, e.g. *entsinnen* [ɛnzɪnn̩] (line 6b), *hatten* (line 14b), *fünfzig* (line 16b), *ganze* (line 17a), *direkten* (line 27b), etc.

(d) Omission of glottal stop. The sharp onset for morpheme-initial vowels generally does not occur in rapid speech except after pause, e.g. lines 4a, 26a, 27a, 29a, 30a, 38a, and occasionally elsewhere when a stressed vowel is set off for clarity, as in line 4b, *Ernst.*

(e) Loss of aspiration. In the discussion of phonotactics (Chapter 7), it was pointed out that in voiceless stop clusters, only the second stop is released, e.g. *Markt, Abt,* etc. In connected speech, however, voiceless stops in word-final position are not released when occurring before an initial lenis. The explosive phase (release) is effected only after the lenis:

Ernst da [ʔɛɐ̯nstd̥a]   (lines 5a, 6a)
ich hab das [çhapd̥as]   (line 7a)

As a whole, aspiration tends to become weaker in rapid speech. In the transcription of Text II, aspiration is marked only when the voiceless stop occurs at the beginning of a syllable with sentence accent or after pause.

(f) Geminate simplification. Geminate consonants, those long consonants which arise due to vowel loss and assimilation, may be simplified in rapid speech, for example, the long or geminate nasals [ŋŋ̩], [mm̩] in:

zeigen	/tsaɪgən/ → [tsaɪgŋ̩] → [tsaɪŋŋ̩] → [tsaɪŋ]	(line 10b)
gegangen	/gəgaŋən/ → [g̊əgaŋŋ̩] →[g̊əgaŋ]	(line 23b)
kommen	/kɔmən/ → [kʰɔmm̩] → [kʰɔm]	(line 40b)

(g) Phonemic stops realized as fricatives. In rapid speech, the realization of stops as voiced fricatives, especially intervocalically, is the result of a loss in articulatory precision: the articulators fail to make a complete occlusion, resulting instead in friction. It could also be viewed as a kind of assimilation to the more open articulation of adjoining vowels. Examples:

hab ich /hɑ:b(ə) ɪx/ → [hɑßɪç] (line 28b) [ß] =bilabial voiced fricative

da [da] → [ða] (line 6b) [ð]=voiced interdental fricative, as in English the.

(h) Centralization of vowels. Also in the category of loss in articulatory precision is the centralizing tendency of vowels in unstressed position, noted briefly in the discussion of Text I. In presto speech, underlying tense vowels in unstressed position may be reduced to [ə]:

Original	/o:ri:gi:nɑ:l/ → [ʔɔɣɪgɪnɑ:l], [ɔɣɪgəna:l]	(lines 12a,b)
Interessent	/ɪntərɛsɛnt/ → [ʔɪntəɣɛsɛnt], [ɪntəɣəsɛnt]	(lines 25a,b)
reflektiert	/re:flɛkti:rt/→[ɣɛflɛktʰi:ɐt], [ɣəflɛktʰi:ɐt]	(lines 27a,b)

11.3.2 Assimilation. In the discussion of Text I, we observed progressive assimilation of voicing, which also occurs in a number of instances in Text II:

*mit*gegeben	[tg̊]	(line 6a)
*ent*sinnen	[tz̥]	(line 6a)
hab das	[pd̥]	(line 7a)
das Blatt	[sb̥]	(line 7a)

In addition, there is one instance of complete assimilation:

das so /das zo:/ [dasso] or [das:o] (line 12a)

Progressive assimilation involving the point of articulation occurs in two places in the presto version of Text I. In Text II this kind of assimilation is far more abundant, especially the assimilation of final nasal to the preceding consonant:

*mit*geg*e*ben	[-bm̩]	(line 6a)
*zei*gen	[-gn̩]	(line 11a)
*e*ben	[-bm̩]	(line 13a)
*direk*ten	[-kn̩]	(line 27b)

Total assimilation is found in:

*Rahm*en	[-mm̩]	(line 19b)
*gegang*en	[-ŋŋ̩]	(line 23a)
*Kund*en	[-nn̩]	(line 27b)
*and*eren	[-n:-]	(line 24b)

Regressive assimilation, assimilation from right to left, occurs in rapid, informal speech. The assimilation of a stop to a homorganic nasal occurs frequently, especially in the auxiliary verb *haben*, e.g. lines 2b, 24a; it also occurs in *eben* (line 13b). The process can be summarized as follows.

		ə-Loss + homorganic assimilation		Regressive assimilation in manner of articulation
/hɑːbən/	→	[hɑːbm̩]	→	[hɑːm]
/eːbən/	→	[eːbm̩]	→	[eːmm̩]

Regressive assimilation at the point of articulation also occurs in:

*mit*gegeben	/mɪtgəgeːbən/ → [mɪkg̊əgeːbm̩]		(line 6b)
*kaput*tgegangen	/kapʊtgəgaŋən/ → [kapʰʊkg̊əgaŋŋ̩]		(line 23b)
fünf	/fʏnf/→[fʏmf], [fʏɱf],		(line 16b)
	[ɱ]= labiodental nasal		

11.3.3 Weak forms. The so-called weak forms encompass those word classes which are usually unstressed in continuous speech—articles, pronouns, prepositions, conjunctions, auxiliary verbs, and others usually labeled 'adverbs' (although such a term obscures a number of essentially different word classes). Some of the same reduction phenomena discussed in 11.3.1 are found among the weak forms, especially elision and vowel centralization. Examples from Text II are outlined here. A complete list of weak forms with all possible reductions is given in Appendix 4.

The forms are given in order of increasing speed and informality from left to right.

(a) Pronouns
   Centralization of vowels:

wir	/viːr/→[viɐ̯], [vɪɐ̯], [vɐ]	(line 9)
Sie	/ziː/→[zi], [zɪ], [zə]	(line 2)
mir	/miːr/→[miɐ̯], [mɪɐ̯], [mɐ]	(line 5)
Ihnen	/iːnən/→[inən], [in:], [ɪn]	(line 10)

Ihrer /iːrər/→[iɣɐ], [ɪɣɐ]   (line 5)
ihn /iːn/→[in], [ɪn], [ən]   (line 21)
Elision
ich /ɪç/→[ç]   in phrase-initial position (lines 7,8,
                                     26,29,32,33,37)
es /ɛs/→[əs], [s]   (lines 7, 10, 20).

(b) Articles
Elision:
ein /aɪn/→[n]   (lines 18, 19)
eine /aɪnə/→[nə]   (line 17)
Centralization of Vowels:
der /deːr/→[deːr],[deɐ̯],[dɐ]   (line 31)

(c) Conjunctions
Centralization of vowels:
wie /viː/→[vi],[vɪ]   (line 12)
and reduction in consonantal articulatory precision (i.e. the full
stop closure is not made):
aber /aːbər/→[aːbɐ],[abɐ],[aßɐ]   (line 27)
oder /oːdər/→[oːdɐ][odɐ],[ɔdɐ],[ɔɾɐ]   (line 9)
                      [ɾ] = dental flap as in
                      American English *city*
Elision:
und /ʊnt/ →[ʊn]   (lines 4, 14)

(d) Prepositions
Centralization of vowels and reduction in consonantal articulatory
precision:
über /yːbər/→[ybɐ]→[ʏbɐ]→[ʏßɐ]   (line 32)
Elisions:
im /ɪm/→[m]   (line 12)
von /fɔn/→[fn̩]   (line 31)

(e) Auxiliary verbs
Length reduction of the vowel, reduction in consonantal articulatory precision:
habe /haːbə/→[habə]→[haß]   (lines 33, 34)
Elision:
ist /ɪst/→[ɪs].   (lines 4,8)

(f) Others
Centralization of vowels:
her /heːr/→[heɐ̯]→[hɛɐ̯]   (line 31)
Vowel shortening, reduction in consonantal articulatory precision:
da /daː/→[ða]   (line 6)

Vowel shortening and elision:
mal   /mɑ:l/→[mal]→[ma]   (line 11)
also   /alzo:/→[alzo]→[azo]   (line 27)
Elision:
nicht /nɪçt/→[nɪç]   (line 19)
jetzt /jɛtst/→[jɛts]   (line 20)
and centralization:
sonst /zɔnst/→[zɔns]→[zəns]   (line 27)

Sentence phonetics remains an area of investigation in which a number of unsolved problems remain. In this chapter a few of the basic concepts and many of the reduction phenomena which characterize spoken German have been examined. Without this aspect of the phonetics, our picture of the language would be incomplete and distorted.

Further reading

Most of the material in this chapter is based on:

Kohler, Klaus J. 1977. Einführung in die Phonetik des Deutschen. Chapter 6. Berlin: Schmidt.
Meinhold, Gottfried. 1973. Deutsche Standardsprache. Lautschwächungen und Formstufen. Jena: Friedrich-Schiller-Universität.

Further discussion can be found in:

Vater, Heinz, ed. 1979. Phonologische Probleme des Deutschen, Tübingen: Narr.

The concept of 'weak forms' was first developed for English in:

Jones, Daniel. 1956. Outline of English Phonetics, 8th ed. Cambridge: Heffer. 126-37.

Problems

Problem 1. What further examples can you find in Text II to supplement the discussion which follows it?

Problem 2. The following is a continuation of Text II. Complete the transcription for presto-style speech.
A: Ich weiß nicht, ob Sie das wußten: Meine Frau war eine Zeitlang berufstätig, und jetzt ist sie im Augenblick nicht mehr. Da bliebe etwas mehr übrig.
S: Ja, klar. Also 2 950 war der Erscheinungspreis jetzt. Und wenn Sie sich dazu entschließen wollen und können, könnten Sie's also auch zu diesem Preis über dies Abzahlen haben.

A single word often betrays
a great design.

—*Racine*

Chapter 12
Morphophonology

12.0 Introduction. As noted in Chapter 6, the phonological rules medi-
ate between the phonemic representation (the 'input') of morphemes and
their respective phonetic outputs. The varying phonetic shapes of the
same underlying morpheme are called allomorphs. For example, the morpheme /me:r/ *Meer* has two allomorphs, [me:ɐ] and [me:ʀ-]. Which one
occurs depends on the phonetic environment: when a vowel follows the
final /r/, the phonetic realization is [me:ʀ-], e.g. *Meere, Meeres;* with no
vowel following, the form is [me:ɐ], e.g. *Meer.* Here the different allomorphs of /me:r/ are correlated with different phonetic realizations of the
phoneme /r/.

In Chapter 6 there is one instance, however, where the phonetic output
results in allomorphs where the alternation is identical to segments already established for the phonemic inventory: the alternation of fortis
and lenis obstruents. Thus, /bɑ:d/ *Bad* has two allomorphs [bɑ:d-] and
[bɑ:t], where the output of the Fortition Rule gives a segment [t] which is
identical to a segment already established by minimal pairs for the
phonological system. The phonemes /t/ and /d/ contrast in all environments except before syllable boundary. In that environment the contrast
is neutralized in favor of the fortis obstruent. When two phonemes alternate in the same morpheme, the alternation is termed 'morphophonemic'.

Whether, now, we have to do with examples such as *Meer-Meere,* where
the allophones [ɐ] and [ʀ] alternate, or with *Bad-Bäder,* where [t] and [d]
alternate, it is the phonetic environment alone which accounts for the alternation. However, alternation of two phonemes in the same morpheme
may also be due to other than the phonetic environment. In this chapter
several instances of this kind of morphophonemic alternation in German
are considered briefly.

137

12.1 Umlaut. In pairs such as *Rat-Räte, Rad-Räder, Vater-Väter, Nagel-Nägel, Grab-Gräber,* etc., the phonemes /ɑ:/ and /ɛ:/ alternate. The alternation is linked to a grammatical marker, the plural, and hence the alternation is GRAMMATICALLY CONDITIONED whenever it occurs (note that there are some nouns which have /ɑ:/ in both singular and plural, e.g. *Ader, Haar, Mal, Schal,* etc.). What is predictable here is that if /ɑ:/ does alternate with another phoneme, it is always /ɛ:/. The same alternation occurs in derivations as well, e.g. adj. *klar,* verb *klären;* noun *Jahr,* adj. *jährlich;* verb *abschlagen,* adj. *abschlägig.* The term 'umlaut' has traditionally been used for this type of morphophonemic alternation. In addition to the /ɑ:/-/ɛ:/ alternation, the following also occur.

/u:/ and /y:/	Fuß-Füße-(bar)füßig
/ʊ/ and /ʏ/	Luft-Lüfte-lüften
/o:/ and /ø:/	groß-größer-größten
/ɔ/ and /œ/	Korn-Körner-körnig
/a/ and /ɛ/	falle-fällst-fällt
/ɑʊ/ and /ɔy/	Haus-Häuser-häuslich-(zwei)häusig

Umlaut is thus the fronting of nonfront vowels, the feature 'round' remaining the same (cf. Table 12.1).

Table 12.1 'Umlaut': The fronting of back vowels.

Front		Central	Back	
−round	+round		−round	+round
	/y:/ ◄———————————			/u:/
	/ʏ/ ◄———————————			/ʊ/
	/ø:/ ◄———————————			/o:/
	/œ/ ◄———————————			/ɔ/
/ɛ://ɛ/ ◄—		——/a/		
			/ɑ:/	
/ɔy/ ◄———————————				/ɑʊ/

Table 12.1 shows that the two low vowels are raised to the next highest level on which front, unrounded vowels occur. The 'backing' diphthong /ɑʊ/ alternates with the 'fronting' diphthong /ɔy/.

From the foregoing examples it can be seen that the morphophonemic alternation known as 'umlaut' occurs in conjunction with four morphological processes: (1) pluralization of nouns; (2) the formation of comparative and superlative; (3) in the second and third person singular present tense of certain verbs; also in Subjunctive II of certain verbs; (4) in derivation (suffixes, such as *-ig, -lich,* etc.). The degree of regularity with which the fronting of nonfront vowels occurs is summarized in Tables 12.2 and 12.3.

Table 12.2 Umlaut as a grammatical marker.

Grammatical category	Associated morpheme	Degree to which umlaut occurs Examples:	
Plural	/-ər/ /-ə/ fem. masc. neut. zero	Always Very few exceptions Varies considerably Very rarely Rarely	Häuser Hände Bäche Flöße Äpfel
Comparative/ Superlative	/-ər/ /-əst/	Only in the following: alt, arm, dumm, grob, groß, hart, hoch, jung, kalt, klug, krank, kurz, lang, nah, oft, scharf, schwach, schwarz, stark, warm Sporadically in the following: bang, blaß, fromm, gesund, glatt, karg, krumm, naß, rot, schmal	
Verb forms: (a) Strong 2nd & 3rd person sg. present indicative	/-st/ /-t/	Few exceptions	trägst trägt
(b) Subjunctive II of strong verbs:	/-ə/ /-əst/ /-ət/ /-ən/	Always	trüge trügest trüget trügen
(c) Modals and subjunctive II of irregu- lar verbs:	(/-t-/)/-ə/ /-əst/ /-ət/ /-ən/	In the following verbs: können, mögen, müssen, dürfen, bringen, denken, brennen, kennen, rennen, brauchen, sein, tun, haben	

Umlaut is a case of the fronting of nonfront vowels in particular morphological environments (plural markers, comparatives, etc.). Two other sets of morphemes show morphophonemic alternation, where the relationship among the alternating phonemes is not, however, reducible to a simple formula such as 'fronting'. Rather, the alternations are functions of particular classes of lexemes. Some linguists use the term MORPHOLEXICAL to describe this kind of alternation. It is found in the 'strong' or ablauting verbs and associated nouns, where various vowel phonemes alternate, and in the alternation of consonants in certain lexemes of foreign origin.

Table 12.3 Umlaut in derivations.

Derivation	Associated morpheme	Degree to which umlaut occurs Examples:
Noun from adjective	/-ə/	Always: Bläue, Güte, Größe
Adjective from adjective	/-lɪx/	Few exceptions: bläulich, zärtlich
Collective noun	/gə-/ . . . (/-ə/)	Few exceptions: Gehäuse, Gelände, Geläuf
Diminutive of nouns	/-xɛn/ /-laɪn/	Few exceptions: Stäbchen, Häuschen Händlein, Brüderlein
Noun from verb	/-lɪŋ/	Few exceptions: Säugling, Sträfling
Iterative or diminutive of verbs	/-l-/	Few exceptions: fädeln, tröpfeln
Adjective from noun	/-bɑːr/	Sporadically: dämpfbar, stürmbar
Feminine noun	/-ɪn/	Sporadically: Hündin, Rätin, Närrin
Agent noun from verb	/-ər/	Frequently: Käufer, Händler
Adjective from noun or verb	/-lɪx/	Sporadically: ärztlich, käuflich
Noun from noun or adjective	/-nɪs/	Frequently: Bündnis, Fäulnis
Adjective from noun	/-ɪg/	Sporadically: gnädig, körnig, bärtig
Adjective from noun	/-ɪʃ/	Sporadically: höhnisch, zänkisch
Verb from noun	/-ən/	Sporadically: küssen, pflügen, ästen

12.2 Ablaut. No phonological conditions can predict which vowels alternate in a set such as *singen-sang-gesungen-Gesang,* or in *bitten-bat-gebeten-Gebet.* The most one can do is to point to certain phonological characteristics which typically cooccur with particular vowel alternations, but there is no question of devising phonological rules.

Approximately 175 'strong' verbs show ablaut. Approximately 85% can be grouped into eight classes. The eight groups are as follows, classified according to the vowel alternation in the present, preterite, and past participle.

1. (40 verbs)
Present: /aɪ/
Preterite and past participle: /ɪ/ before fortis
                       obstruents
                       /iː/ elsewhere
Examples: beißen-biß-gebissen
           bleiben-blieb-geblieben
           leihen-lieh-geliehen
           scheinen-schien-geschienen

2. (25 verbs)
Present: /ɪ/
Preterite: /a/
Past participle: /ʊ/ before /ŋ/ and nasal + consonant
                /ɔ/ elsewhere
Examples: singen-sang-gesungen
           binden-band-gebunden
           beginnen-begann-begonnen

3. (19 verbs)
Present: /iː/
Preterite and past participle: /ɔ/ before fortis
                       fricative
                       /o/ elsewhere
Examples: fließen-floß-geflossen
           biegen-bog-gebogen
           fliehen-floh-geflohen
           verlieren-verlor-verloren

4. (19 verbs)
Present: /eː/, /ɛː/ before sonorant
          /ɛ/ elsewhere
Preterite: /ɑː/ before single consonant
          /a/ elsewhere
Past participle: /oː/ before single liquid
                /ɔ/ elsewhere

Examples: brechen-brach-gebrochen
    bergen-barg-geborgen
    stehlen-stahl-gestohlen

5. (15 verbs)
Present: /e:/, /ɛ:/ before lenis stops and /r/
   /ɛ/ elsewhere
Preterite and past participle: /o:/ before lenis
          stops and /r/
         /ɔ/ elsewhere
Examples: bewegen-bewog-bewogen
    scheren-schor-geschoren
    fechten-focht-gefochten

6. (10 verbs)
Present and past participle: /a/ before fortis
           obstruent
       /ɑ:/ elsewhere
Preterite: /u:/
Examples: wachsen-wuchs-gewachsen
    graben-grub-gegraben

7. (9 verbs)
Present and past participle: /ɛ/ before /s/
       /e:/ elsewhere
Preterite: /ɑ:/
Examples: vergessen-vergaß-vergessen
    lesen-las-gelesen

8. (7 verbs)
Present and past participle: /a/ before /l/ and /s/
       /ɑ:/ elsewhere
Preterite: /i:/
Examples: fallen-fiel-gefallen
    blasen-blies-geblasen
    raten-riet-geraten

Some verbs, such as *sieden, leiden, schneiden* and *ziehen,* not only show morphophonemic alternation among the vowels, but also have unique alternations among the medial consonants as well. These belong to that 15% which cannot be classified under the foregoing scheme.

12.3 Consonant alternation. Certain consonant phonemes, primarily obstruents, alternate in some words of foreign origin, e.g. /b/ and /pt/ in *absorbieren* and *Absorption*. A phonological rule of /s/-insertion occurs regularly when an ending beginning with /i:/, such as *-ion, -iös, -ios,* is added to a lexical morpheme ending in /t/, as in the case of *Absorption* (pronounced [ʔapzɔ̯ɐptsi̯oːn]). The following examples are arranged without considering the automatic insertion of /s/. Hence, in a pair, such as *Perfekt-perfektion,* there is actually no morphophonemic alternation, since both have /pɛrfɛkt/ in common.

Alternation	Examples

1. Obstruent alternating with zero:

ø /t/	exerpieren Exzerpt
	rezipieren Rezept
ø /s/	frequentieren Frequenz
	Konkurrent Konkurrenz
	Präsident Präsidenz

2. Alternation of obstruents:

/b/ /pt/	absorbieren Absorption
	transkribieren Transkription
	subskribieren Subskription
/d/ /z/	elidieren Elision
	applaudieren Applaus
/g/ /kt/	fungieren Funktion
	reagieren Reaktion Reaktor
	korrigieren Korrektur
/t/ /s/	dissentieren Dissens
	komprimittieren Kompromiß
	diskutieren Diskussion
/ts/ /k/	musizieren Musik
	provozieren Provokateur
/ts/ /kt/	produzieren Produkt Produktion
	projizieren Projektor
	infizieren Infekt Infektion
	infektiös Infektiosität

3. Alternation of sonorant and fricative

/n/ /z/	komponieren Komposition
	Komponist
	transponieren Transposition

Further reading

For a rather advanced, general treatment of the subject matter, cf.:

Dressler, Wolfgang. 1977. Grundfragen der Morphonologie. Wien: Verlag der österreichischen Akademie der Wissenschaften.

For a discussion of the distinction between 'morphophonemic' and 'morpholexical', cf.

Matthews, P. H. 1972. Inflectional morphology: A theoretical study based on aspects of Latin verb conjugation. Cambridge: Cambridge University Press.

Problem

The morphophonemic alternation known as 'umlaut' shows regular fronting of nonfront vowels whenever the proper morphological conditions are present. Can you formulate this process in terms of a phonological rule? Where do the difficulties lie? If it were entirely regular, would not the 'umlaut' of /ɑʊ/ be [ɛʏ]? Why do you think this is not the case?

Exercises:
The sounds of German

I. Vowels.

On the accompanying tape you will hear examples of the vowel sounds of German, illustrated with material found in Chapter 2. We will proceed in the order of the discussion taken up there, first treating the high and mid tense and lax vowels, then the low vowels, the mid-central vowels, the diphthongs, and finally, the nasalized vowels.

Tense and lax vowels. These sounds are all monophthongs, that is, they are pronounced without tongue movement. The stressed tense vowels are on the average longer than the auditorily similar English vowels, whereas the lax vowels are somewhat shorter than the auditorily similar English lax vowels. Each example will be repeated three times.

2.2.1. The high vowels.

[i:] high, front, tense, long, unrounded.
initially: Igel, ihn
medially: lieb, Lied
finally: Vieh, Biologie
For comparison, auditorily similar English words will be pronounced alongside German *Igel, Lied* and *Vieh:*

German: Igel	English: eagle
Lied	lead
Vieh	fee

American speakers typically make two related errors: (1) their German [i:] is diphthongized, i.e. the tongue moves from a somewhat lower position up to [i]; this is especially noticeable in final position; (2) the vowel is too short.

To help correct these problems, spread the lips exaggeratedly, tense the muscles of the tongue and jaw (using a mirror here, as always, is a useful

145

check) and make the sound extremely long. The exaggerated muscular tension and length will gradually give way to a more natural articulation once you have become accustomed to the different muscular movements the German sounds require. Listen and repeat:

Igel - ihn - lieb - Lied - Vieh - Biologie

[ɪ] high, front, lax, short, unrounded.
initially: ist, in
medially: Kinn, Sinn
finally: no examples

Auditorily, this vowel sound resembles that in English *in* and *kin*. The chief problem for American speakers is the tendency to make the vowel too long and somewhat diphthongized. The easiest corrective is to move to the following consonant as quickly as possible. Listen to the difference between German and English:

German: in   English: in
      Kinn   kin

In Chapter 4, section 4.3, the two high, front vowels [i:] and [ɪ] are contrasted. Listen to the difference between them:

[i:]	[I]
Miene	Minne
siezen	sitzen
Miete	Mitte

[u:] high, back, tense, long, rounded.
initially: Uhr, U-Boot
medially: Hut, Mus
finally: Kuh, Schuh

For comparison purposes, auditorily similar English words will be pronounced alongside German *Hut, Mus, Kuh* and *Schuh:*

German: Hut   English: hoot
      Mus   moose
      Kuh   coo
      Schuh   shoe

As with the high, front tense [i:], American speakers tend to diphthongize the German vowel as well as to render it too short. Similar corrective measures suggested above can be applied here. The lips should be strongly rounded (check in a mirror), the muscles of the jaw and tongue tense in order to prevent movement of the tongue, and the vowel articulated exaggeratedly long. Repeat from the tape the following list:

Uhr - U-Boot - Hut - Mus - Huh - Schuh

[ʊ] high, back, lax, short, rounded.
initially: und, unter
medially: Bus, Busch
finally: no examples

Auditorily, this sound resembles that in English *book* and *bush*. Again the tendency of American speakers is to lengthen and diphthongize the vowel. A conscious effort must be made to make the vowel as brief as the one you hear on the tape. Listen to the difference between German and English:

German: Busch   English: bush
      kuck'   cook

In Chapter 4, section 4.3, the two high back vowels [u:] and [ʊ] are contrasted. Listen to the difference between them:

[u:]	[ʊ]
Ruhm	Rum
spuken	spucken
Mus	Muß

[y:] high, front, tense, long, rounded
initially: üben, über
medially: kühl, Typ
finally: früh

Since there is no auditorily similar sound in English, the pronunciation of this vowel poses particular problems. The first step is to be comfortable with the long, tense [i:]. Once you have gotten the feel for articulating [i:] exaggeratedly long and without tongue movement, [y:] requires only the added component of lip-rounding. Start by pronouncing the above words as if they had [i:] rather than [y:] in them. Then, after pronouncing, for example, [i:bən] several times, round the lips and try saying [i:bən] again. The result should be [y:bən] 'üben'. It is essential that you 'think' [i:] while rounding the lips to prevent lapsing into a back vowel. Practicing in front of a mirror will allow visual control of lip-rounding. Listen and repeat:

üben - über - kühl - Typ - früh

[ʏ] high, front, short, lax, rounded
initially: üppig
medially: Fürst, dünn
finally: no examples

Since the difference between [ɪ] and [ʏ] is one of lip-rounding, the same procedure can be applied as for the tense vowel. Practice, for example, the nonsense syllable [dɪn]. Then round the lips and attempt the same syllable. The result should be [dʏn] 'dünn'. Again, it is helpful to 'think' [ɪ] while articulating [dʏn], to prevent lapsing into a back vowel. Listen and repeat:

üppig - Fürst - dünn

In Chapter 4, section 4.3, the two high, front, rounded vowels [y:] and [ʏ] are contrasted. Listen to the difference between them:

[y:]	[ʏ]
fühlen	füllen

Fühler   Füller
Hüte   Hütte

2.2.2. The mid vowels.

[e:] mid, front, tense, long, unrounded.
initially: edel, eben, Ehre
medially: Lehm, Mehl, Beet
finally: See, Reh
For comparison, auditorily similar English words will be pronounced
alongside German *Lehm, Mehl, See* and *Reh:*

German: Lehm	English: lame
Mehl	mail
See	say
Reh	ray

American speakers typically make two related errors: (1) their German
[e:] is quite diphthongized, i.e. the tongue moves from [e] to approximately [i]; (2) the vowel is too short.

Moreover, when the vowel occurs before German /r/, the tongue is typically too low, approximately [ɛ].

To help correct these problems, spread the lips exaggeratedly, tense the
muscles of the tongue and jaw (using a mirror is a helpful check) and make
the sound [e:], as at the beginning of *edel,* exaggeratedly long. The exaggerated muscular tension (to prevent tongue movement) and length will
gradually give way to a more natural articulation once you have become
accustomed to the muscular movements which [e:] requires. When articulating a word such as *Ehre,* begin by pronouncing the initial vowel as if it
were that in *Ehe;* pause and then articulate the trill plus schwa: [e:] + [ʀə].
Subsequently, articulate the vowel + trill with shorter and shorter pauses
until you can articulate the vowel without lowering the tongue. Listen and
repeat:
   edel - eben - Ehre - Lehrer - Mehl - Beet - See - Reh

[ɛ] mid, front, lax, short, unrounded.
initially: essen, Ecke, Äpfel
medially: Fell, leck hält
finally: no examples
Auditorily, this vowel sound resembles that in the name of the English letter 's' and *fell.* The chief problem for American speakers is the tendency to
make the vowel too long and somewhat diphthongized. Try to imitate the
brevity of the vowels you hear on the tape. Listen to the difference between German and English:

German: essen	English: (the letter) 's'
Fell	fell

[ɛ:] **mid, front, lax, long, unrounded.**
initially: Ähre
medially: Bär, träfe
finally: zäh
Although this sound resembles the vowel in English *at*, the tongue does not drop quite that low. It is simply a longer version of the vowel in German *Fell*. Listen and repeat:
Ähre - Bär - träfe - zäh

[o:] **mid, back, tense, long, rounded.**
initially: Ohr, Ohm, Ostern
medially: Sog, Lob, tot
finally: so, roh, floh
Auditorily, this vowel resembles that in English *tote, so* and *flow*, with the difference, however, that the German is a monophthong. The English vowel tends toward diphthongization, that is, the tongue moves from [o] to approximately [u], a tendency especially noticeable in final position. For comparison, auditorily similar English words will be pronounced alongside German *Ohm, tot* and *floh:*

German: Ohm	English: ohm
tot	tote
floh	flow

As with the other tense vowels, the tendency toward diphthongization and incorrect length can be remedied by tensing the muscles of the tongue and jaw and articulating the sound in isolation before a mirror. Then try imitating the following words:
Ohr - Ohm - Ostern - Sog - Lob - tot - so - floh

[ɔ] **mid, back, lax, short rounded.**
initially: Ost, Ort, Opfer
medially: rollen, Tonne, Torte
finally: no examples
For most speakers of American English, there is no auditorily similar sound. The German sound tends to be replaced either by the vowel sound in *coast* or that in *ton* or *stop*. An initial approximation to German [ɔ] can be achieved by articulating the vowel in English *ton* but with rounded lips. A mirror is essential to ensure that rounding occurs. Practice on the following words, where the usual tendency is to replace German [ɔ] with the vowel in English *ton* or *stop*. Note especially that the German vowel, like all lax vowels, is very short:
Tonne - komm- Sonne - stop - Mop - Dock
Listen to the difference between German [ɔ] and auditorily similar vowels in English:

German: Tonne	English: ton
komm	come

Sonne	sun
stop	stop
Mop	mop
Dock	dock

Repeat the following words, rounding the lips *before* attempting to articulate the word as a whole:

Tonne - komm - Sonne - stop - Mop - Dock

[ø:] mid, front, tense, long, rounded.
initially: öde, Öfen, Öhre
medially: König, töten, Bögen
Finally: Bö

Once you have the feel for articulating [e:] without diphthongizing it, [ø:] will follow fairly easily. It requires only lip-rounding in addition. Start by pronouncing the above examples as if they had [e:] rather than [ø:] in them. Then, after pronouncing, for example, [e:də] several times, round the lips strongly and try saying [e:də]. The result should be [ø:də] 'öde'. Listen and repeat:

öde - Öfen - Öhre - König - töten - Bögen - Bö

[œ] mid, front, short, lax, rounded.
initially: öfter, östlich, örtlich
medially: Hölle, möchte, völlig, können
finally: no examples

Since the difference between [ɛ] and [œ] is one of lip-rounding, the same procedure can be applied as for the tense vowel. Practice, for example, the nonsense syllable [ɛst]. Then round the lips and attempt the same syllable. The result should be [œst] (as in *östlich*). Again, render this vowel very short. Listen and repeat:

öfter - östlich - örtlich - Hölle - möchte - völlig - können

In Chapter 4, section 4.3, the two mid, front, rounded vowels [ø:] and [œ] are contrasted. Listen to the difference between them:

[ø:]	[œ]
Höhle	Hölle
Röslein	Rößlein
Schöße	schösse

2.2.3. The low vowels. Short [a] and long [ɑ:] are distinguished as to length.

[a] low, central, short.
initially: alle, As, an
medially: Fall, Faß, kann
finally: no examples
Listen and repeat:

alle - As - an - Fall - Faß - kann

[ɑ:] low, back, unrounded, long.
initially: Aale, Aas, Ahn
medially: fahl, las, Kahn
finally: na, sah
Listen and repeat:
Aale - Aas - Ahn - Fahl - las - Hahn - na - sah
Note the distinction in length in the following pairs:

[a]	[ɑ:]
alle	Aale
As	Aas
an	Ahn
Fall	fahl
kann	Kahn

2.2.4. The mid central vowels [ə] and [ɐ]. The first of these two vowels, the schwa, has an exact counterpart in English. In German, it occurs in unstressed syllables only. Examples:

The final sound in: Rute, Ruhe, liege, lade;
The first sound in: gemacht, Gewächs, betont.

The second mid-central vowel, symbolized by the upside-down 'a', is articulated with the apex of the tongue touching the gums below the lower incisors. Use a mirror as a check. Holding the tongue in this position will prevent the production of an American 'r'-sound (which requires the tongue tip to be raised toward the alveolar ridge).

Listen to the final sound in the following words:
bitter, größer, eher, Mieter.
Listen to the following pairs of words, in which schwa contrasts finally with the other mid-central vowel:

bitte	bitter
Größe	größer
ehe	eher
Miete	Mieter

Now repeat the following pairs:

bitte   - bitter
Größe - größer
ehe   - eher
Miete - Mieter

2.2.7. Diphthongs. Each of the three diphthongs in German has a close English counterpart. The chief problem for American speakers is making the diphthongs too long, especially in final position. Listen to the following three sets, where the diphthong occurs finally:

[aɪ]	Mai	sei	Weih
[aʊ]	Sau	Frau	lau
[ɔy̆]	Neu	Heu	scheu

Now repeat:
Mai - sei - Weih
Sau - Frau - lau
neu - Heu - scheu

2.2.8. Nasalized vowels. These vowels are articulated with the velum down. Listen to the following examples:
Teint - Bon - Parfum - Gourmand
Now repeat:
Teint - Bon - Parfum - Gourmand

II. Consonants

On the accompanying tape you will hear examples of the consonant sounds of German, illustrated with material found in Chapter 3. We will proceed in the order of the discussion found there.

3.1 Stops. Since German and English stops are for all intents and purposes articulated in the same way, no major problems arise in learning the German stops. In German, however, all stops are released, whereas American English speakers often do not release stops in word-final position. Concentrate on the final stops in the following words:
knapp
stop
tot
hat
leck
Trick
Now repeat:
knapp - stop - tot - hat - leck - Trick

3.2. Fricatives. The fricatives at the labial and alveolar positions are so similar to English fricatives that no further discussion is necessary.

[ʃ] dorsoprepalatal fortis. There are two major differences between the German and the auditorily similar English fricative: (1) The German fricative is articulated with strongly rounded lips; (2) a larger volume of air is blown through the vocal tract. A mirror is essential for ensuring that the lips are rounded, and a conscious effort at articulating the [ʃ] with greater energy must be made. Listen to the following items:
initially: schon, schicken, Schuh
medially: Asche, mischen, tuschen
finally: fesch, Tisch, Fleisch
Repeat:
schon - Schuh - Asche - mischen - Tisch - Fleisch

[ʒ] dorsoprepalatal lenis. In isolated words this sound is heard voiced. The lips are rounded, but considerably less energy is required (and hence

less air) is required than for [ʃ].
initially: Journal, Giro, Genie
medially: Etage, Loge, Regie
finally: no examples
Repeat:
Journal - Giro - Genie - Etage - Loge - Regie

[ç] dorsopalatal fortis.
initially: Chemie, China
medially: Seuche, Kirche, Leiche
finally: ich, euch, Milch, König
The major difference between this sound and the prepalatal [ʃ] is two-fold: (1) the lips are spread; (2) the surface of the tongue is flat (for [ʃ] it is grooved). There are a couple of exercises the English-speaker can perform to master this sound. One is to pronounce English words such as 'hit' and 'him' with an exaggeratedly long initial consonant and with audible breathiness. Then try adding [ɪ] before initial [h] to form nonsense words [ɪhɪt], [ɪhɪm], etc. When you have a good rendition of a very long, breathy 'h', eliminate the final syllable and you should have a fairly acceptable [ɪç] 'ich'.
A second exercise consists of raising the tongue slowly from the [ɪ] position with the intention of forming a stop at the hard palate. First place the tongue in the position for [ɪ], then whisper it and raise it toward the palate. As the tongue approaches the palate, [ç] will be heard.
Listen and repeat:
Chemie - China - Seuche - Kirche - Leiche - ich - euch - Milch - König

[j] dorsopalatal lenis. The major difference between the German sound and the auditorily similar English sound heard initially in 'yes' is that the German is articulated with somewhat more energy.
initially: ja, je, Jodel
medially: Major, Boje
finally: no examples.
Listen and repeat:
ja - je - Jodel - Major - Boje

[x] dorsovelar fortis.
initially: no examples
medially: mache, faucht, tauchst, Bucht, Sache
finally: Buch, doch, hoch, auch
A couple of exercises enable the English-speaker to master this sound in German. One consists of breathing in and out rapidly (panting) and gradually raising the back of the tongue so that it approaches the velum and friction is created. A second consists of repeating the nonsense syllables [aka] and gradually loosening the constriction formed by [k] with each repetition. The result will be [axa].

Listen and repeat:
mache - faucht - tauchst - Bucht - Sache - Buch - doch - hoch - auch

[ɣ] dorsovelar lenis. We will forego a treatment of this sound until the discussion of the trill.

3.3. The vowel onsets. [h] requires no special comment since it is articulated the same as the English sound.

The glottal stop [ʔ] is heard at the beginning of stressed syllables beginning with a vowel. Listen to the following examples:
initially: ein, alt, Auto
medially: Verein, Theater, uralt
Since glottal stop occurs in American English before the vowels in 'uh-uh', it is a question of transferring this articulatory habit to German vowels.
Listen and repeat:
ein - alt - Auto - Verein - Theater - uralt

3.4. The nasals. The nasals are articulated identically to those in English.

3.5. The lateral [l].
initially: Leiter, laden, los
medially: Meile, Keller, Eule
finally: hell, heil, Greuel
In German the tongue is kept flat in the mouth except for the apex, which touches the alveolar ridge. The tongue is approximately in that position for the English lateral when adjacent to high, front vowels. Practice an exaggeratedly 'bright' [l] in words such as 'million', 'hilly', 'billions'. Once you have a feel for the position of the tongue, try the same with the German lateral in the same environment: *Stille, Stühle, Iltis.* The tongue position for [l] in German adjacent to [l] is the same for all phonetic environments, whereas in English the back of the tongue tends to be raised especially in the environment of back vowels. Listen to the difference between the German lateral after a back vowel and the English:

German:		English:	
	Polen		poling
	Hallen		hauling
	Stuhl		stool
	Kultur		culture

Listen and repeat:
Polen - Hallen - Stuhl - Kultur

3.6. The trill:
initially: Ruhm, rennen, Ring, Rost
medially: fahre, Meere, Marine, größere
finally: no examples
A first approximation at a uvular trill can be achieved by tilting the

head back and gargling (note that the vocal bands vibrate). Initially, one can practice nonsense syllables in this position, e.g. [ɑːʀə], [oːʀə], etc. Then the same exercise can be tried without tilting the head back. The exercise can then be varied so as to eliminate the initial vowel, e.g. [ɑːʀə] - [ʀə], etc. Gradually, the necessity of expending a great deal of energy will decrease. After this sound and [x] have been thoroughly mastered, the use of [ɣ] in colloquial contexts can be attempted; [ɣ] is [x] with voice added. It requires less expenditure of energy than for either [x] or [ʀ].

If you have already learned to articulate the apical [r] and use it effortlessly, you may want to consult your instructor concerning the feasibility of using it rather than switching to the uvular trill.

Appendices

Appendix 1 Long vowels before two or more tautosyllabic consonants.

(1) Before /st/:

düster	Ostern
hüsteln	plustern
husten	pusten
Kloster	Rüster
Knust	trösten, Trost
Österreich	wüst, Wüste, Wust

Also short: Nüster, rösten, Schuster

(2) Before /tʃ/:

ätsch	Kartätsche, kartätschen
Bratsche	Latsch
Grätsche, grätschen	latschen, latschig
hätscheln	rätschen, ratschen
Karbatsche, karbatschen	watscheln

(3) Before /r/ plus alveolar obstruent:

Art, artig	Quarz, quarzig
Erde	(du) wärst
Harz	(ihr) wart
Pferd	

Also short: Arzt, Ärztin, Arznei, Barsch, Erz (mineral), Schwarte

(4) Before other consonant clusters:

Jagd	Magd
Keks	Mond
Koks	Obst
Lotse	Papst

Propst   Vogt
Rätsel   Wuchs, wuchs, wüchsig

Appendix 2 Long vowels before <ch> and <sch>.

brach (verb)   Kuchen
brach (adj.)   nach (except where weakly stressed)
Brache   nächst
Buch   Ruch
Buche   Schmach
Fluch, fluchen   sprach
Gemach, Gemächer   Sprache
gemächlich   stach
Gespräch, gesprächig   suchen
hoch, höchst   Tuch
Huchen   Wucher
Also short: Bruch (swamp)

Liesch(e)
Nische
Rüsche
wusch
Also short: Dusche

Appendix 3 Examples of words with [ʒ].

Blamage   Jongleur
Courage   Journal
engagieren   Loge
Etage   logieren
Flageolett   Massage
Garage   Menage
Gelatin   Menagerie
Gelee   menagieren
Gendarme   Page
Genie   Pagerie
genieren   Passage
Gilet   Prestige
Giraffe   Rage
Giro   Regie
Ingenieur   Regime
Jackett   Regisseur
Jalousie   Reportage
Jargon   Spionage

Stellage   Vernissage

Examples of words with [dʒ].

Adagio   Jockey
Budget   Judo
Dschungel   Magenta
Gin   Maggio
Jab   Maharadscha
Jam   Management
Jazz   Manager
Jeep
Job

Appendix 4 Sentence phonetics: Weak forms.

Pronouns:
ich   [ɪç] →[ç]
mir, dir, ihr, wir   [-iɐ̯]→[-ɪɐ̯]→[-ɐ]
du   [du]→[də]
er   [eɐ̯]→[ɛɐ̯]→[ɐ]
ihm   [im]→[ɪm]→[əm]→[m]
ihn   [in]→[ɪn]→[ən]→[n],[m],[ŋ]
sie   [zi]→[zə]
ihre(s,r)   [iʁə(s)]→[ɪʁə(s)],[iʁɐ]→[ɪʁɐ]
ihren, ihrem   [iɐ̯n],[iɐ̯m]→[ɪɐ̯n],[ɪɐ̯m]
es   [(ə)s]
ihnen   [inn̩]→[in]→[ɪn],[ɪm],[ɪŋ]

Articles:
der   [deɐ̯]→[dɛɐ̯]→[dɐ]
des   [dəs]
dem   [dem]→[dɛm]→[dəm]→[dm]→[m]
den   [den]→[dɛn]→[dən]→[dn]→[n],[m],[ŋ]
die   [di]→[dɪ]→[də]
das   [s]
ein(en)   [ən]→[n],[m],[ŋ]
einem   [nəm]→[m]; [aɪ̯m] →[am]
einer   [nɐ]
eine   [nə]
dessen   [dəsn̩]
deren   [deɐ̯n]→[dɛɐ̯n]
denen   [denn̩]→[den]→[dɛn]→[dən]

Auxiliary verbs:

bist	[bɪs]
ist	[ɪs]→[s]
sind	[zɪn]
werden	[veɐ̯n]→[vɛɐ̯n]
wurden	[vʊɐ̯n]
würden	[vʏɐ̯n]
geworden	[gəvɔɐ̯n]
habe	[haßə]
haben	[ham]
soll	[sɔ]
will	[vɪ]

Prepositions:

über	[ʏbɐ]→[ʏßɐ]
zu	[tsʊ]→[tsə]
von	[fən]→[fn̩]
vor	[foɐ̯]→[fɔɐ̯]→[fɐ]
für	[fyɐ̯]→[fʏɐ̯]→[fɐ]
nach	[nax]
in	[ən]→[n],[m],[ŋ]

Conjunctions:

und	[ʊn]→[ən]→[n],[m],[ŋ]
aber	[aßɐ]
oder	[odɐ]→[ɔdɐ]→[ədɐ]
wie	[vi]→[vɪ]
da	[da]

Adverbs:

nicht	[nɪç]
jetzt	[jɛts]→[jəts]
sonst	[zɔns]→[zəns]
denn	[dən]→[dn̩]→[n̩]
so	[zo]→[zɔ]→[zə]
schon	[ʃon]→[ʃɔn]→[ʃən]→[ʃn̩]
nun	[nun]→[nʊn][nən]
nur	[nuɐ̯]→[nʊɐ̯]
mal	[ma]

Numerals ending in -zehn:

[-tse:n]→[-tsen]→[-tsɛn]→[-tsən]→[-tsn̩].

(From Klaus J. Kohler, *Einführung in die Phonetik des Deutschen*, pp. 224-25; reproduced by permission of the Erich Schmidt Verlag).

Symbols and abbreviations

C   any consonant
V   any vowel
Ø   zero, no segment
Ç   diacritic above or below a consonant symbol indicates that the sound is voiceless, e.g. [b̥], [g̊]
Ç Ć   diacritic above or below a consonantal sonorant symbol indicates that the sound is syllabic, e.g. [n̩],[n̩].
[ ]   symbol between square brackets represents a sound or phone
/ /   symbol between slashes represents a phoneme or underlying segment of the language
V: colon following the symbol indicates that the sound is long
V·   raised dot following the symbol indicates that the segment is half-long
ˈ   raised vertical stroke indicates primary stress on the following syllable; used in phonetic transcriptions
V́   phonetic stress mark indicates primary stress when the word is written in standard orthography, e.g. árbeite.
V̀   grave accent mark indicates secondary stress
V̯   indicates nonsyllabic vowel
*   unacceptable or nonoccurring form in the language
→   means 'is realized as'; the segment to the left of the arrow is realized as the segment(s) to the right of the arrow
/   a slash means 'in the phonetic environment of', e.g. /V____ means 'in the environment following a vowel'
a double cross signifies a word boundary, e.g./____# means 'in the environment before a word boundary,' i.e. at the end of a word
+   morpheme boundary, e.g. Tage can be divided into two morphemes: /tɑ:g+ə/
.   a period represents a syllable boundary, e.g. Tage is divided /tɑ:.gə/
‖   boundary between tone groups
//   pause

Glossary

Ablaut. The alternation of stressed vowels in the same morpheme. In German, ablaut characterizes the strong verbs and their related nouns and adjectives, e.g. *werfen/wirft/warf/geworfen/Wurf; beißen/biß/gebissen/bissig/Biß.*

Acoustic phonetics. That branch of the science of sound which investigates the physical properties of speech sounds, such as pitch, amplitude, and frequency.

Affricate. An obstruent consisting of a stop followed by a fricative. The clusters [pf], [ts], and sometimes [tʃ] are referred to as affricates in some descriptions of German.

Allegro. Cf. Presto.

Allophone. A speech sound which is one variant of a phoneme. An allophone may be a positional variant of a phoneme, e.g. German [ɐ], which is the realization of /r/ after a vowel; or it may be in 'free' variation, as when either [ɐ] or [ɣ] occurs after a lax vowel before consonant.

Antepenultima. The third-to-last syllable in a word. In *Rhinózeros,* for example, primary stress falls on the antepenultimate syllable. Cf. also ultima and penultima.

Articulatory phonetics. That branch of the science of sound which investigates the production of speech sounds in the vocal tract.

Aspiration. Airflow through the vocal tract which results from a delay between the release of the occlusion and the onset of voicing of the following vowel. In German, aspiration accompanies /p/, /t/, /k/, when these are realized tautosyllabically before a stressed vowel.

Assimilation. A phonetic process which occurs when one segment becomes like another due to a change in one or more features. Assimilation can be partial, as when /b/ is assimilated in voicing to the preceding voiceless consonant, as in *das Bett* [das b̥ɛt]. It can also be total, as when a final nasal /n/ assimilates completely to a preceding /m/, resulting in [m:], as in [kʰɔm:] from /kɔmən/.

Auditory phonetics. That branch of the science of sound which investigates the hearing and perception of speech; sometimes called 'psychological phonetics' or 'psychophonetics'.

Bilabial. A sound articulated by closure of the lips, e.g. /p/, /b/, /m/, or partial closure, e.g. [ß].

Closed syllable. Syllable ending in one or more consonants, e.g. German *stumm, Stumpf.*

Coda. That part of the syllable following the peak, e.g. /m/ in *stumm,* /mpf/ in *Stumpf.*

Commutation. If two linguistic entities, for example, phonemes, can occur in the same linguistic environment, and hence are interchangeable, they are said to be commutatable.

Complementary distribution. Refers to the distribution of allophones in mutually exclusive environments, e.g. German [x] after nonfront vowels [ç] elsewhere.

Consonant. A sound produced by offering some impedence to the stream of air passing through the vocal tract. Consonants are subclassified into obstruents and consonantal sonorants.

Contrast. Two sounds are contrastive if they can be used to distinguish otherwise identical word pairs, e.g. /k/ and /g/ in *Kasse:Gasse.*

Deletion. Loss of a segment. The term is sometimes used in the context of phonological rules, as when /ə/ is deleted before final /r/, e.g. /bɛkər/ [bɛkɐ]. Deletion may also occur in rapid speech, as when the /t/ of /axt/ 'acht' is lost before the /t/ of /-tse:n/ in 'achtzehn'.

Demonstrative. In German, words such as *dieser, der, jener, derselbe, derjenige,* etc., used to point out particular persons or things.

Determiner. A class of words which occurs before the noun in German, such as articles, possessives, demonstratives, quantifiers, and numerals.

Diphthong. A vowel sound produced by movement of the tongue from one point to another in the 'vowel space', e.g. [aɪ], [aʊ], [e:ɐ], etc.

Distinctive. Those features of phonemes which are responsible for forming contrasts are distinctive, e.g. fortis and lenis in German.

Distinctive features. Any phonetic characteristic used to distinguish classes of phonemes from one another. The feature [−cont], for example, distinguishes /p t k b d g m n ŋ l/ from all other phonemes of German.

Elision. The loss of sounds between syllable peaks, e.g. /ə/ in *geschlossenen* /gəʃlɔsənən/ → [gəʃlɔsnən].

Feature matrix. A table giving the values for the distinctive features of the individual phonemes.

Fortis. A sound produced with high airflow and greater muscular tension, e.g., /p/, /t/, /k/ in German. Contrastive term: Lenis.

Fricative. A consonantal sound produced by blowing the air from the lungs through a narrow aperture in the oral cavity, resulting in noisiness, e.g. the initial sound in *fett* and *satt.*

Glottis. The space between the vocal cords. When the vocal cords are apart, the glottis is said to be open. When the vocal cords lie adjacent to one another, the glottis is said to be closed.

Height or Tongue height. Relative position of the tongue on a vertical axis. Traditionally, tongue heights are designated as high, mid, and low.

Homophonous words. Words having the same sequence of sounds, e.g. *Waise, Weise, weise.*

Homorganic. Refers to the same place of articulation; for example, /p/, /b/, and /m/ are all homorganic.

Indefinite pronoun. One of a group of words whose referent is not specific, e.g. *jemand, niemand, jedermann, keiner,* etc.

Interlude. The consonant or consonants between syllabic peaks, e.g. /m/ in *Sommer,* /nd/ in *Bundes.*

Intervocalic. Between vowels. The /b/ in *aber* and *Eber* is intervocalic.

Intonation. A melodic pattern of pitch differences occurring during a stretch of speech.

Lateral. An oral sound produced by blowing the airstream around the edge (latus) of the tongue.

Lax. A descriptive category for vowels. Lax vowels are characterized by the tongue being relatively less retracted from the 'neutral' ([ə]) position than the tense vowels. The lax vowels in German are [ɪ ʏ ʊ ɛ œ ɔ].

Lenis. A sound produced with low airflow and little muscular tension, e.g. /b/, /d/, /g/ in German. Contrastive term: Fortis.

Lento. Relatively slow, careful speech style.

Lexeme (or Lexical morpheme). A morpheme which is the main carrier of meaning, as opposed to grammatical morphemes and derivational morphemes (suffixes).

Liquids. A cover term for the nonnasal sonorants /l/ and /r/.

Major class features. In distinctive feature theory, these are 'consonantal', 'syllabic', and 'sonorant'.

Minimal pairs. Pairs of words in a language which differ by only one phoneme.

Monophthong. A vowel sound produced with no movement of the tongue during its articulation.

Morpheme boundary. The 'seam' between two morphemes; it can also designate the beginning or the end of a morpheme. Usually marked with a '+', e.g. *arbeit + s + los.*

Nasal. A sound produced by lowering the velum, allowing the air to escape unhindered through the nasal passage. Blockage occurs in the oral cavity. Contrast: Oral.

Nasalization. The quality given to a sound by allowing the air to escape through the nasal cavity. Vowels in a limited number of words in German are nasalized when the velum is lowered while the tongue is in position for the articulation of the vowel.

Neutralization. The canceling of a phonological opposition. The best-known example is the neutralization of the fortis-lenis distinction at the end of syllables in German.

Nuclear syllable. That syllable in an utterance marked by sentence accent and change in pitch.

Obstruent. A consonantal sound produced by blowing the air through a restriction in the vocal tract. The velum is up and the air passes through the center of the oral cavity. Obstruents are subclassified into stops, fricatives, and affricates.

Onset (or **Syllable onset**). That part of the syllable preceding the peak, e.g. /ʃt/ in *stumm.*

Open syllable. Syllables ending in a vowel, e.g. German *nah, le(ben), klei(ne).*

Opposition. Refers to the entities, e.g. phonemes of a language which contrast with one another, e.g. /m/ vs. /n/, /t/ vs. /d/, etc.

Paralinguistics. The study of those features of speech which characterize individuals or which are not readily susceptible to rule, such as pause and tempo.

Peak. The peak of a syllable is the most sonorous sound, usually a vowel, but it can also be a syllabic consonant, as in the final sound of *Hebel.*

Penultima. The second-to-last syllable in a word. In *interessíeren* and *Rhododéndron,* for example, the penultimate syllable has the word stress. Cf. also Ultima and Antepenultima.

Phonation. The action of the vocal cords in the production of speech. One of the four speech processes, the others being the airstream process, the oronasal process (position of the velum) and the articulatory process (tongue and lips).

Phonological rule. A linguistic device for relating the underlying or phonemic level of analysis to the phonetic level, that of actual pronunciation.

Plosive. Alternative term for 'stop'.

Prenuclear syllable. That syllable in an utterance which precedes the nuclear syllable, e.g. *du* in *Kommst du mít?* where *mit* is the nuclear syllable.

Presto (Allegro). Relatively rapid style of speaking.

Prosody. A cover term for intonation, sentence accent, pause, and other phenomena which usually occur over stretches of speech. Cf. also Suprasegmental.

Retraction or Tongue retraction. Relative position of the tongue on the horizontal (front-back) axis (front=palatal region; back=velar region).

Rhythm. The organization of stresses and syllables into groups, analogous to the metric feet in poetry.

Rounded. Sounds are rounded which are produced with the corners of the lips drawn toward the center. The lips may be 'pursed' or thrust forward to various degrees, e.g. lip rounding is more pronounced for the articulation of [u] than for [ɔ].

Segment. Any linguistic unit abstracted from actual speech, e.g. a phoneme, phone, etc.

Sonorant. A class of sounds characterized by a relatively unobstructed vocal tract. It includes vowels, nasals, laterals, and trills.

Sonority. The quality of a sound, such as loudness, which makes it more prominent than adjacent sounds. Sonority depends on the state of the vocal tract and on the quality of the adjacent sounds. Vowels are the most sonorous sounds (open vocal tract), obstruents the least.

Spirant. Alternative term for 'fricative'.

Spread. Sounds are spread or nonrounded when the corners of the lips are not drawn together, but remain as in a position of rest. Contrastive term: Rounded.

Stop. A consonantal sound produced by blocking the airstream from the lungs by the formation of a complete closure in the oral cavity. It is a manner feature of consonantal production, consisting of three phases: (1) movement of the articulators together; (2) occlusion; (3) release.

Stress. That part of an utterance which receives greater prominence in comparison to contiguous parts. Generally, stress is referred to that syllable of a word which is perceived as the loudest. In *Antwort,* for example, the initial syllable is stressed; in *Café,* the second syllable is the more prominent.

Suprasegmental. A cover term for intonation, sentence accent, pause, and other phenomena which usually occur over stretches of speech. The term refers to those characteristics which are, so to speak, 'superimposed' on a string of segments (phonemes). More recently, the term 'prosody' has been favored by many linguists.

Syllabic consonant. Those consonants /m n ŋ l r/ which can function as syllable-forming sounds, e.g. the /l/ in *Tafel* [tʰɑːfl̩].

Syllable boundary. The designation given to that point which divides two syllables. The period in *frag.te, Tan.go* and in *ba.den* represents a syllable boundary in these words.

Tautosyllabic. Occurring within the same syllable. In *spannt,* /n/ and /t/ are tautosyllabic, whereas in *Kienteer,* /n/ and /t/ belong to different syllables.

Tense. A descriptive category for vowels. Tense vowels are characterized by the tongue's position being further retracted from the 'neutral' ([ə]) position than the lax vowels and inherently longer. The tense vowels in German are [iː yː uː eː øː oː].

Text. In linguistics, a text may be either spoken or written, and refers to a number of connected utterances which form a coherent whole.

Tone group. In prosodic theory, a stretch of speech dominated by one nuclear syllable.

Trill. An oral sound produced by a rapid repetitive movement of the apex against the alveolar ridge, or of the uvula against the dorsum, in German, [r] and [ʀ], respectively.

Ultima. The last syllable of a word. In *Biologie* and *interessánt*, for example, the ultima is stressed. Cf. also Penultima and Antepenultima.

Umlaut. In morphophonology, a term for the fronting of nonfront vowels in particular morphemes. In orthographical discussion, it refers to the two dots (also called a 'trema') over the vowels *ä, ö, ü.*

Vowel. Speech sound produced with no stricture in the vocal tract above the glottis. In German, all vowels are voiced.

Vowel onset. Refers generally to [h] and [ʔ].

Vowel space. That part of the oral cavity in which all the vowel sounds are articulated.

Zusammenrückung. A type of compound formed by joining members of small classes of words, such as prepositions, determiners, and adverbs.

References

Anderson, Stephen R. 1974. The organization of phonology. New York: Academic Press.

Bibliographie zur Phonetik und Phonologie des Deutschen. 1971. Tübingen: Niemeyer.

Borden, Gloria J., and Katherine S. Harris. 1980. Speech science primer. Physiology, acoustics and perception of speech. London, Baltimore: William & Wilkins.

Chomsky, Noam, and Morris Halle. 1968. The sound pattern of English. New York: Harper & Row.

Dinnsen, Daniel A. 1979. Current approaches to phonological theory. Bloomington: Indiana University.

Dressler, Wolfgang. 1977. Grundfragen der Morphonologie. Wien: Verlag der österreichischen Akademie der Wissenschaften.

Duden. Fremdwörterbuch. 1966. Der große Duden, 2. Aufl. Band 5. Mannheim, Wien, Zürich: Dudenverlag.

Duden. Aussprachewörterbuch. 1974. Der große Duden, 2. Aufl., Band 6. Mannheim, Wien, Zürich: Dudenverlag.

Essen, Otto von. 1964. Grundzüge der hochdeutschen Satzintonation. 2. Aufl. Ratingen: A. Henn.

Fremdwörterbuch. 1964. Leipzig: VEB Bibliographisches Institut.

Germanistik. Internationales Referatenorgan mit bibliographischen Hinweisen. 1960-. Tübingen: Niemeyer.

Halle, Morris, and G. N. Clements. 1983. Problem book in phonology. Cambridge, Mass.: MIT Press.

Heike, Georg. 1972. Phonologie. Stuttgart: Metzler.

Herbst, Thomas, David Heath, and Hans-Martin Dedering, eds. 1979. Grimm's grandchildren. Current topics in German linguistics. London and New York: Longmans.

Hooper, Joan B. 1976. An introduction to natural generative phonology. New York: Academic Press.

Isačenko, Alexander, and Hans-Joachim Schädlich. 1970. A model of standard German intonation. (Janua linguarum, series practica 113.) The Hague: Mouton.

Jakobson, Roman, Gunnar M. Fant, and Morris Halle. 1951. Preliminaries to speech analysis: The distinctive features and their correlates. (3rd printing 1963.) Cambridge, Mass.: MIT Press.

Jakobson, Roman, and Morris Halle. 1956. Fundamentals of language. s'Gravenhage: Mouton.

Jones, Daniel. 1956. Outline of English phonetics. 8th ed. Cambridge: Heffer.

Kallmeyer, Werner. 1981. Aushandlung und Bedeutungskonstitution. Dialogforschung. Jahrbuch 1980 des Instituts für deutsche Sprache. Edited by Peter Schröder and Hugo Steger. Düsseldorf: Schwann. 89-127.

Kenstowicz, Michael. 1979. Generative phonology. New York: Academic Press.

Kohler, Klaus J. 1977. Einführung in die Phonetik des Deutschen. Berlin: Schmidt.

Kreuzer, Ursula, and Klaus Pawlowski. 1971. Deutsche Hochlautung. Stuttgart: Klett.

Ladefoged, Peter. 1971. Preliminaries to linguistic phonetics. Chicago and London: University of Chicago Press.

Ladefoged, Peter. 1975. A course in phonetics (2nd ed. 1982.) New York: Harcourt Brace Jovanovich.

Lehiste, Ilse. 1970. Suprasegmentals. Cambridge: MIT Press.

Linell, Per. 1979. Psychological reality in phonology. A theoretical study. Cambridge: Cambridge University Press.

MacCarthy, Peter. 1975. Pronunciation of German. London: Oxford University Press.

Martens, Carl. 1966. Abbildungen zu den deutschen Lauten. 2. Aufl. München: Hueber.

Matthews, P. H. 1972. Inflectional morphology: A theoretical study based on aspects of Latin verb conjugation. Cambridge: Cambridge University Press.

Meinhold, Gottfried. 1973. Deutsche Standardsprache. Lautschwächungen und Formstufen. Jena: Friedrich-Schiller-Universität.

Meinhold, Gottfried, and Eberhard Stock. 1980. Phonologie der deutschen Gegenwartssprache. Leipzig: VEB Bibliographisches Institut.

Mendelssohn, Peter de. 1977. Ein Schriftsteller in München. Thomas Mann 1875-1975. Edited by Beatrix Bludau, Eckhard Heftrich and Helmut Koopmann. Frankfurt: S. Fischer. 5-32.

Moulton, William G. 1962. The sounds of English and German. Chicago: University of Chicago Press.

Pheby, John. 1975. Intonation und Grammatik im Deutschen. Berlin: Akademie-Verlag.

Philipp, Marthe. 1974. Phonologie des Deutschen. Stuttgart: Kohlhammer.

Pulgram, Ernst. 1970. Syllable, nexus, cursus. The Hague: Mouton.

Scholz, Hans-Joachim. 1972. Untersuchungen zur Lautstruktur deutscher Wörter. München: Fink.

Schulz, Hans. 1913-. Deutsches Fremdwörterbuch. (3 vols.) Berlin, New York: Walter de Gruyter.

Siebs. Deutsche Aussprache. 1969. Berlin: Walter de Gruyter.

Sommerstein, Alan H. 1977. Modern phonology. Baltimore: University Park.

Stampe, David. 1979. A dissertation on natural phonology. Bloomington: Indiana University Linguistics Club.

Stock, Eberhard, and Christina Zacharias. 1973. Deutsche Satzintonation. Leipzig: VEB Bibliographisches Institut.

Stötzer, Ursula. 1975. Deutsche Aussprache. Leipzig: VEB Verlag Enzyklopädie.

Textor, A. M. 1969. Auf deutsch. Das Fremdwörterlexikon. Hamburg: Rowohlt.

Trubetzkoy, N. S. 1969. Principles of phonology. Berkeley: University of California Press.

Vater, Heinz, ed. 1979. Phonologische Probleme des Deutschen. Tübingen: Narr.

Wängler, Hans-Heinrich. 1974. Grundriß einer Phonetik des Deutschen. 3. Aufl. Marburg: Elwert.

Wängler, Hans-Heinrich. 1972. Instruction in German pronunciation. (3rd ed.) St. Paul: EMC Corp.

Werner, Otmar. 1972. Phonemik des Deutschen. Stuttgart: Metzler.

Wörterbuch der deutschen Aussprache. 1969. 2. Aufl. München: Hueber.

Wurzel, Wolfgang Ulrich. 1970. Studien zur deutschen Lautstruktur. (Studia grammatica 8.) Berlin: Akademie-Verlag.

Index